UP CHUTE CREEK

An Okanagan Idyll

"For 30 years, my family has made a ritual pilgrimage to celebrate food's seasonality by picking cherries in the Okanagan Valley, the Garden "of Eatin" of this book. But in that time, the rural charm of this area has changed beyond recognition from the forces of development and growth. Up Chute Creek zip-lines readers through this region's environmental issues, from population growth and water shortage to a unique, but endangered ecology. No easy solutions, but what a ride!"

— DAVID SUZUKI, AUTHOR OF THE SACRED BALANCE AND
HOST OF CBC'S THE NATURE OF THINGS

View of Okanagan Lake south from the Granite Farm.

MELODY HESSING

Up Chute Creek

An Okanagan Idyll

OKANAGAN INSTITUTE
2009

LIBRARY AND ARCHIVES CANADA CATALOGUING IN PUBLICATION
Up Chute Creek: An Okanagan Idyll.
ISBN 978-0-9810271-1-1
A catalog record for this publication is available from the
National Library of Canada.

Publisher and designer: Robert MacDonald
Editorial advisors: Harold Rhenisch and Luanne Armstrong
Front cover painting: Jack Davis
Photos: Melody Hessing and Jay Lewis
Watermark: Frances Hatfield and Tricia Burtch
Printed in Canada by Houghton Boston

PRODUCED AND PUBLISHED BY THE **OKANAGAN INSTITUTE**
1473 Ethel Street, Kelowna BC V1Y 2X9 Canada
www.okanaganinstitute.com

10 9 8 7 6 5 4 3 2 1

CONTENTS

PREFACE

The Okanagan Mountain Park fire bookends this narrative. Building a house in a 'fire zone' creates a dynamic connection between men and women, urban and rural lifestyles, and humans and the natural world. In this humorous tale of 'post-urban neo-ruralism', ties with community and environment shape a life in the South Okanagan.
Up Chute Creek is a story of "landscaping" — the ways you forge connections to a place as it creeps into your bones and shifts the geography of your soul.

When I moved to Naramata B.C. in the early 1970's, stucco motels, benchland orchards and fun-in-the-sun tourism were the main ingredients of the South Okanagan lifestyle. Today 'wine country' includes estate wineries, golf courses, casinos, cycling trails, and triathlons, attracting residents and tourists alike to a diversity of upscale venues and activities. Yet there are few published accounts of the ways in which rapid growth, diminished biodiversity, and social change have shaped the contemporary South Okanagan. This story provides a glimpse of the Okanagan region in transition, celebrating its unique character and contributing to its cultural heritage.

Landscapes include the ways we change the land, and the ways that the land changes us. How do we — any of us — reconcile development with preservation, past with present, neighbors with friendship, and marriage with autonomy, youth with age? Life in the Okanagan is shaped by an indigo lake and sun-baked clay bluffs, the geometry of vineyards, and the blast-furnace heat of dry summers. This environment frames our everyday lives, but it is a background whose features we sometimes forget. Themes of urban/rural tension, gender relations, community, economic transition, and declines in biodiversity may be relevant throughout Canada, but in the Okanagan we experience them in an exceptional social and ecological context.

I moved to the Okanagan Valley in 1974. Late-comers to the back-to-the-land movement, my husband and I built an unobtrusive house by hand on a rocky cliff near Naramata. Young and naïve like many others, we ignored the (dis)connects between romantic ideals and rural pragmatism, topography and age. Following a quarter century of coming and going home-away-from-home, I remain tethered to the vulnerability and beauty of this arid, rocky landscape.

This narrative is about the continuing 'development' of this province – the spill of people into place, and how the place and the people change.

MELODY HESSING
Naramata 2009

Melody Hessing has taught Sociology, Women's Studies and Environmental Studies at Okanagan College and other post-secondary colleges and universities in British Columbia, and currently teaches at the University of British Columbia. She has published two books (UBC Press) as well as numerous popular and academic articles on topics ranging from environmental policy to ecofeminism. More recently, her creative non-fiction stories have been published in several anthologies; she was a 2008 finalist in the CBC Literary Awards.

Chute Creek in spring run-off.

PART ONE
Foundations

At any location on earth, as the rock record goes down into time and out into earlier geographies it touches upon tens of hundreds of stories, wherein the face of the earth often changed, changed utterly, and changed again, like the face of a crackling fire.

– JOHN MCPHEE, ANNALS OF THE FORMER WORLD

... the physical features of any and all landscapes are construed through the cultural assumptions of the viewer.

– SUSAN R. SCHREPFER, NATURE'S ALTARS

AUGUST 28, 2003

FIVE HUNDRED METRES FROM THE FRONT PORCH, the sparse ponderosa forest has been bulldozed into a dust bowl. With each footstep my boots disappear into smoky swirls of silt. Tire tracks flounder in all directions, marked by limp streamers of neon pink flagging tape.

The Okanagan Mountain Park Fire has burned for over a week, destroying 250 square kilometers of forest and 239 homes. Today the evacuation order has been rescinded, and I have come home. The once familiar landscape is reduced to black and white, to nightmare trees and ashen soil. The plants I know — juniper, currant, wild rose and saskatoon — have been obliterated. Black pincushions of bunchgrass tuft the ground like dryland sea urchins. Ashtray lichen crackles under my feet; curlicues of lacy grass turn to dust in my hand. Where tree roots once burrowed for moisture, dinosaur tracks post-hole the earth like the catacombs of an ancient civilization.

The pine forest is a moonscape purged of green, a negative of itself. This is groundtruth. This is what happened here.

❧ 1 ❧
Exploration

*They came out as a challenge ... the young Englishmen didn't know what the hell
they were coming out to in the first place. They just imagined a sort of beautiful
halo around everything ... I guess I was one.*

– PADDY ACLAND, IN MITCHELL AND DUFFY, BRIGHT SUNSHINE
AND A BRAND NEW COUNTRY: RECOLLECTIONS OF
THE OKANAGAN VALLEY 1890-1914

"Ahh, Vahncoovare," nods the porter at the Montreal West train station.
"Vous avez de la chance!"

But compared to Sainte Catherine's Street, 1969 Vancouver is stodgy,
dull, and repressed, its sobriety reflected in an endless rain drizzling on
stucco bungalows and sodden lawns. On the cusp of metropolis, Vancouver is pouring tea.

Jay and I leave Quebec in the throes of separatism-Francophone versus Anglophone, Ottawa against the provinces, the East bleeding the West,
urban cities trumping rural roots. We've only been married for two years
and the world is falling apart.

Our first pied-a-terre is a motel on Kingsway, with mustard-hued
fridge and stove, and pea-green curtains. Its double bed is mired in thick
custard shag, sporting a bedspread of autumn riot – yellow, orange, red

and brown. The room smells like curried pastrami. It's like living in a pizza.

We move downtown, to a 12th floor one-bedroom apartment on Alberni Street. The living room wall is glass, opening to a view of the high-rise West End, featuring the 24-hour drama of the Super Valu parking lot just below and behind our building. The rain erases mountains; the fog clouds English Bay.

We've moved west to see a new world, explore new country, and get a new start. During the next year, Jay tries a succession of jobs. He works for an alternative paper and free-lances as a writer. I enroll in the Ph.D. program at UBC and teach Sociology at Capilano College. My part-time job is gut-wrenching – all that driving through the city, over the bridge, and back home. Even the traffic is constipated.

On the weekends we escape to the dry Interior of the province. Just 300 kilometers from the sea, the sunny rain shadow of the Cascades sears the rolling hills that berm Okanagan Lake. Up mountains and down valleys, we inhale hillsides of sunflowers and soft sagebrush. Tracing the flow of the Similkameen, we turn north into the Okanagan Valley, where open rangeland is corralled into tree fruit plantations that stick like cloves in a Christmas ham. Osoyoos, Vaseux, Skaha, Okanagan, Kalamalka: the name of each lake is like water slaking our thirst.

Every week, more people are moving 'back to the land' – to Powell River, Fauquier, Cherryville, and Kaslo. In the early seventies, British Columbia is a Whole Earth Catalog of alternative lifestyles. Communes and cooperative ventures offer collective approaches to relationships, housing, and community. Feminism, deep ecology and the peace movement promote egalitarian, environmentally sound ways to live. We join a food co-op. Jay writes for 'Poppin', a 'counter-culture' rag, and I take dance classes every day at the Paula Ross studio on Broadway (Dum, bah bah, Uum bah bah, da da da da DUM!) But the hinterland of British Columbia exerts the strongest pull. In 1970, just over two million people inhabit this province. You can still hear the call of the wild.

We are drawn to the Okanagan Valley, especially the South Okanagan, which is hot, arid and sparse in both population and vegetation. For weeks we consider the McCuddy Ranch, on the road up to Mount Baldy east of Oliver: one hundred hectares, with an old, decrepit red farmhouse, seedy meadows and patches of lodgepole pine. It's a "needs work" kind of place. You can imagine an entire commune settling in, with new buildings hatching, meadows ploughed into gardens, and puffs of smoke encircling the house from a rusty cook stove. Rusting in the pasture you'd see a couple of pick up trucks, a VW van, an ancient Greyhound bus, and the carcass of an old washing machine.

❦

A year later, we're driving up from the city on the Crowsnest Highway, past the Hope Slide. The car clings to the Skaist River as the highway curls through the Cascades. I tense at every curve, my eyes narrowed on the road.

Jay is driving. Out of the corner of his eye, he steals a look at me. "You know, we're not the first ones to think about moving to the Interior."

But I'm wound tight. "I know. Miners used the Dewdney Trail during the Gold Rush over a hundred years ago." I look out the window where the rocky run of the Skagit River races beneath skyscraper cedars, and try to imagine the straggle of men carting their worldly goods into the unknown. I'm not made of pioneer stock.

Later that afternoon, as the car sweeps down from Twin Lakes into Kaleden, I am at the wheel: "I just don't think I could ever live here. It's nice to visit, but I'm not sure about staying here." I floor the gas pedal, and the car lurches into the oncoming lane, squeaking past a Berry and

Smith truck heading north to Penticton.

Scanning the oncoming traffic, Jay reminds me: "Yeah, but we can never even find a campsite when we come up here. We end up staying in cheap motels with paper walls."

My shoulders hunched, I reply: "But when do we ever meet people like us? Under 50? Young people here are dying to move to the city. Everybody we see is at least twenty years older than us...."

Jay looks out the window at the dry hills of the Reserve, at buffalo grazing on the Okanagan Game Ranch, fruit stands boarded up for winter and the gnarled symmetry of winter orchards.

But I'm on a roll. I pull out to pass a car that's barely going the speed limit. "You know what they say, 'Newly wed and nearly dead.' If they're our age, they have children. That'd be me in the veggie patch, kids tugging at my apron strings. You'd be out with the chain saw, buzzing the next cord of wood."

I crank the wheel, and the car squeals back into the northbound lane as a truck screams past on our left, headed south to Osoyoos. "And where would I get a job up here?"

Jay's voice speeds up. "You could teach anywhere in the province! But that's not the point. We'll find jobs. Besides, it will cost us much less to live in the country."

"But these places will become urban too. If we end up in Kelowna, it would be like moving to the suburbs. I grew up in the suburbs!"

He says slowly, as if he's memorized the script. "Remember, we came here to try something different. We're educated and have work experience." He turns to the east, to the mountains above Skaha Lake.

Jay's voice rises. "Pollution is growing, species are going extinct and we're just the tip of Ehrlich's Population Bomb. People are flooding the planet. We've got to find some place that is a place and will stay a place."

❧

At UBC, I'm a teaching assistant for the Introductory Anthropology/ Sociology course. Allison, a student in one of my tutorials, lives on an orchard in Naramata, just north of Penticton. In 1971, the population of Kelowna in the Central Okanagan is 19,000; Penticton, in the South Okanagan, registers 18,000. In Naramata, the current count is 908. One day in class Allison talks about the community where she grew up.

"When my dad broke his leg, at picking time, all the neighbors came over to help. They brought their ladders and trucks over to our place. They were finished faster than if we'd done it ourselves."

I tell the story to Jay. He grins and nods his head.

🦌

Jay is a rural romantic. He subscribes to "Organic Gardening" and devours Rodale's Intensive Organic Primer. He checks his tomato seedlings every day, probably even talks to them.

I love flowers, but I'm not much of a gardener. Real farming means ceaseless physical effort and uncertain rewards. Rootstocks, grafts, thinning and pruning are not in my vocabulary.

Jay tells endless stories about when he was a kid, growing up in a small town: "We'd go over to Farney's barn every chance we'd get, to watch them milk the cows. That warm grassy smell even in the middle of winter, all cozy and steamy, with the cows moaning, and that fresh-cut smell of hay, and the snow piling up outside ..."

I grew up near a city. I dream about bus routes.

🦌

A year later, Jay is the West Coast distributor for Laser sailboats, which he occasionally transports to the B.C. Interior. His dealer in the Okanagan is Alex Tynesworth, a British ex-pat who lives with his wife Jeannie in an old, red clapboard house in Naramata. Alex and Jeannie's kids have already left home, lured to the city by Petula Clarke's 'Downtown,' blasting from Penticton's CKOK 800. Their house is cozy and warm, surrounded by orchards - cherries, apricots, and apples. After dinner, Alex asks, "Did you know that we're thinking of buying some property?"

Jay's eyes light up, and he shifts in his chair.

Alex leans over the hearth, his v-necked sweater cozied by firelight, and chucks another stick of apple prunings into place on the coals. The wood crackles in its own conversation. "It's north of town, several kilometers past the old dump."

Jay sits up.

Alex leans further towards us, his eyes twinkling behind his wire-rimmed glasses. "The property comes with waterfront, a lovely beach, once you get there. Not a great moorage... (A moorage! Worth more than a peerage), but it means not having to drive all the way around to Summerland just to go for a sail."

Jay stretches his legs in front of him; his long body stiffens in the chair. He can barely restrain himself.

Alex continues, "This place is really getting too crowded for us." He looks over towards me as I stand and walk over to the window."They're building new houses right up to the railway line. We can hear our neighbors chatting at night."

I look outside at the black sky, the stars, and the lights in the distance.

"You can see, we're practically surrounded. You must come and have a look." He eases back in his chair and shifts his weight, as if it's already been decided.

I look back out into the void. There is nothing, nobody there.

❦

The next day we are like kids at Christmas, huddled in the back of The Heffalump, the red VW tractor-trailer Alex and Jeannie use to go to the dump. Alex passes the turn to the town of Naramata and continues north, while I jabber excitedly, pulling my jacket tight against the cold. Jay points to rock faces furry with emerald moss. Small creeks thicketed in wild rose furrow each curve in the road. The Lake swallows more and more of the western horizon, until it veers out of sight. We head into oblivion.

As the road tilts downhill past the cattle guard, Alex pulls off to the side. We unfold from the car onto rolling, open grasslands. The freeze-dried air is supercharged with sage, the soil pocked with pebbles and cracked by frost. Ahead, below the rocky rim of Okanagan Mountain, the land plunges into a series of terrace-like benchlands, then plummets down clay banks into the brushed aluminum surface of Okanagan Lake, stretched flat and calm, a mirror of the blue-grey sky. There are no houses, no interruptions, and no sounds.

Alex gestures to the north. "Do you see that bluff rising up from the lake?"

Jay and I gaze up to raggedy ridgeline of Okanagan Mountain – a rough topography of rocky bluffs and canyon walls and scar-faced cliffs staggered by pine and fir.

"Well, down under that ridge is a fifty-acre piece of land for sale."

Arrow-leafed Balsamroot, *Balsamorhizasagittata.*

❦ 2 ❦
Negotiations

My father was all hopped up about a place … called the Okanagan Valley.
Now it was just as simple as that to him, that… you bought a 10-acre orchard
and you made 1000 pounds a year out of it … my idea was riding horses
and hunting grizzly bear … – becoming as wild as possible …We hadn't
the foggiest notion what we were coming out to.

– PADDY ACLAND, IN MITCHELL AND DUFFY, BRIGHT SUNSHINE
AND A BRAND NEW COUNTRY

In 1972, the process of buying land privately is all about having tea. Janie Harris is standing at the front door of her big concrete house, wearing an old flannel shirt, pants and boots. This is a working farm, ranch, and orchard – part cowboy, part colonial, and all geared to maintaining an agricultural enterprise. Sophia Loren à la campagna, with warm brown eyes, chestnut hair and ruddy cheeks, Janie waves us through the front porch and into the kitchen.

The Harrises are originally from Rhodesia, and their big old kitchen is steeped in the clutter and dark of Empire. China cups and a mammoth tea-cozied teapot are soon crowded onto the table. Everett Harris emerges from the nether regions of the house, with a twinkle in his eye, swaths of silver in his hair, and reading glasses that twitch up and down the bridge of his nose in a perpetual reflex motion.

We regale one another with bear stories (the North American equivalent of the safari tale) and then chat about the weather, sports, sailing, and boats –everything but property. Then Everett looks up. "I understand that you've been speaking with Alex."

He looks at us directly, as if seeing us for the first time. "To reach the place, you follow the old Northwood logging road uphill. Once you cross the creek, you can have a look. Here...".

He scrawls an undecipherable map on a napkin and with a flourish, passes it across the table. "This will help. The other possibility is to continue downhill, cross the wooden bridge, and start uphill from there. Either way, you can't avoid climbing."

Everett pushes his chair away from the table, and ambles out of the room. We've been dismissed. Janie wipes her hands on her towel, sees us to the porch and through the door. Nothing more is said about the amount of land for sale, the boundaries, or the asking price.

This February day drizzles with ice-cold sleet. We drive downhill, across the white wooden bridge over Chute Creek, and park the car. Then we scramble up the cliffs along the creek and through a narrow draw where ponderosa and Douglas fir feather the sky. On a small plateau more than 100 meters above the main road, we stop to catch our breath.

To the southwest, the wind-scoured lake puddles in front of us like an enormous turkey platter. Uphill, a rocky amphitheatre scoops scabby granite from a tombstone sky. The entire landscape is a washout, the dregs of winter, glaciers, and gravity. As we shiver in the icy wind, the clouds draw apart in the silver sheen of afternoon. Light streams down in liquid sheets on flaxen stems of bunchgrass, lichened granite and fuzzy green velvet moss, each tiny star sated with moisture. Beneath our feet the first buttercups of spring curl into being.

Jay turns to me, his hazel eyes glinting green and gold in the sun. "It's perfect. We don't have to farm it. We can't farm it. Let's call it The Granite Farm."

🦌

Back in the city, I'm doing research in the dark, musty cavern of the UBC library. After jotting down my references, I descend to the stacks-underground floors with shelves of scholarly journals, volumes of words stifled by weight and the formality of academic presentation. For my Ph.D. in Sociology, I'm conducting research on media coverage of art, studying the ways in which dance and visual arts are reviewed in the print media.

How do you write about something that has no voice? How can you work in a place with no sky?

🦌

"I don't think I'm getting anywhere," Alex confesses, dejected and flat when we see him in March. "Is Everett interested in selling, or not? I've been dithering with him for two years now, and I'm beginning to consider purchasing property closer to town. I'm tired of beating around the bush." If Harris won't sell to Alex, our own purchase will never proceed.

We're back in Alex and Jeannie's living room in Naramata. Wearing his favorite threadbare gray-brown sweater, Jay sips his tea like a modern-day remittance man, supported in the colony until he's learned a trade. I can't get the hang of teacups-the dainty finger hold, the shallow bowl. I grew up with coffee mugs.

Alex deftly replaces his cup on its saucer and sighs, "Do you realize what I've been going through? Once, while I was at the house, trying to speed things up a bit, Everett asked if I played squash.

"It's the dead of winter, one of those dark days when the sun never shines. In that crypt of a house, he leads me downstairs to the basement, where a monstrous old heater cranks away, pipes burrowing into the ceiling. The furnace is enormous, the size of a truck."

He pauses for another sip of tea.

"Waves of heat pulse from the inferno, like Shiva, the Goddess of Destruction. Everett reaches over towards me as I cling to the bottom of the stairs, gaping at the darkness and shrinking from the roar of the heat.

"He hands me a squash racket. Then he promptly rolls up his pants, fires a ball at the wall, and runs to the far side of the room, shouting, 'Yours, Alex'. Well, I am sharp enough to grasp the principle of the thing. I tear across to the other end of the room, around the bloody furnace, and slam the ball back.

"For almost an hour, I dash back and forth across the room, frantic to hit the ball, but even more desperate to avoid being burnt.

"With considerable agility, I keep the ball in play, with rebounds on old boxes, pipes stuck in the corner, old irrigation fittings. I finally give in, finished. I am spent. Everett is triumphant....

Alex pauses, and looks over to us. "So you see, I have paid my dues!"

The next day we drop in at the Harrises at teatime, which spans the entire day. Janie puts the kettle on and Everett, gray wavy hair pushed back, emerges from the depths of the house, disheveled and distracted. He is lithe and quick as a cat; his musings verge from sudden genius to incoherence. After a lengthy preamble, discussing rugby and soccer, wildlife and the weather, he suddenly coughs, then mumbles, "Would you like to take a look at the property lines? I've had a surveyor up. A line of sight is possible from the survey stakes."

The three of us pile into Everett's small truck and hurtle up the old

Northwood road. The truck buckles, spitting rocks and rubble as it gasps uphill. The dogs careen back and forth in the back, then bound from the box as we jolt to a stop on the lip of an old logging bridge.

"As you can see, the creek borders the property," shouts Everett over the din of the waterfall. He strides uphill in gumboots, survey papers rolled under his arm, paying no heed to the twenty-meter cataract of Chute Creek as it cascades into the rock canyon below.

Bringing up the rear, I teeter at the sight of the steep descent, stepping back a few feet from the edge of the tea-stained creek bed. In front of me, Jay is trying to maintain a respectable pace with Everett, while the dogs romp and bark and sniff with abandon. This part of the land is steep, inaccessible, and dangerous. You could slip out of sight here and be lost forever. Nobody would look for you, and even if they did, the chance of finding you would be slim.

Everett turns and points uphill back towards the creek. "There's the upper boundary," he says, motioning vaguely up the steep, sandy hillside.

With that, he turns abruptly and bounds downhill, the barking dogs cutting back and forth in front of him. When we catch up with Everett at the truck, he's already backing around, ready to take off. The dogs are braced in the truck bed. As we lurch downhill, wedging ourselves against the door and one another, Jay bursts out, "Everett, we do need to talk about water..."

Eyes straight ahead, Everett nods. "You must apply separately to the Ministry for water rights, as they do not accrue to the property. But I doubt there will be a problem. "

"How much can we request?" asks Jay.

"It is my understanding that this will not be an agricultural request, granted in acre feet. I assume that you will require domestic use only. This should not pose any difficulty."

Undeterred by this cryptic reply, Jay continues: "Everett, I also want to ask you about road access." He turns, peering over his shoulder, and gestures back up the road. "We're thinking of building the house up there."

The truck springs downhill like a mule deer. Everett continues: "I will do my best to provide road access, but this will be contingent on other projects." We careen downhill.

I look at Jay, raising my eyebrows in a private message. "Yes," I add. "But the view..."

Everett slides the truck into his driveway. "I will attempt to incorporate access when I develop the next set of plans. By the way, do you play tennis? We're setting up a clay court."

❦

The next time we check with Alex, he grins. "You know, Everett stopped at the mailbox to chat with me yesterday. I was wearing this bit of rope as a belt, a piece of the line I use to rig my boat. I always wear it, because I can adapt it to use on the tiller when I go out for a sail.

Jay and I smile in anticipation. He continues, "Everett must have noticed this, because as the car took off he was fumbling with something. He yanked his belt off his own trousers and threw it to me at the side of the road, calling out, 'You need this more than I do.'"

❦

As we traipse uphill, the sunflowers of arrowleaf balsamroot dot the pine-needled hillside. "We have to build a house here!" yells Jay, from behind a big yellow pine on the rocky plateau. Its needles dimple with round droplets of water like mercury in a thermometer, magnifying each tiny green groove. Beneath the ponderosa, a saskatoon droops a leggy calligraphy of blossoms.

Okanagan Lake floods the horizon, its basin flanked to the south by benchlands peppered with orchards and vineyards. Below the road, clay banks erode to hoodoos and cliffs that sugar down to the lake. Across the valley, sandy hillsides swell up to 7,000-foot mountains — Apex and Beaconsfield, Riordan, Brent and Sheep Rock.

The valley stretches to the south in a canopy of sky that billows like a blue parachute above our heads. "You've got to admit that this is the best site. It's flat, it has tremendous views, and it's secluded." Jay has made up his mind.

"That's obvious," I retort, scrambling to join him. "How could anybody get to this place?" I'm out of breath. My jacket, wrapped around my waist, sways its empty arms like the forelegs of a clown horse.

My breath catches up with me. "How do *we* get here? And what about supplies?

"You're always so negative," Jay sighs. He gestures back across the hillside. "We get here like we did today — up the logging road, and across the hill. That way, when you get here you're grounded. You smell the place; you feel it, you hear it. It's part of you. Not just something you drive by."

"But Everett still hasn't signed off on our access."

"He said he would! He included road access to the creek in the sales agreement. It's as good as done."

We are latecomers in the occupation of this place. In the late 1800's miners and ranchers trickled into a valley already inhabited by First Nations, to be followed in the 1900's by a flood of crop farmers and orchardists. On the Harrises' upper bench, tucked behind clumps of aspen, Graham's 60-year old cabin shifts and sags year by year, slowly being absorbed by the earth. Nowadays most undeveloped pieces are steep, rocky and non-arable, 'non-productive' sites where only fools and falls congregate.

The property we're buying is triangular in shape, bounded by Chute

Creek to the south, a seasonal creek to the north, and the public road along the bottom. The sandy, pine-studded grasslands of its lower hillsides climb abruptly to the rocky domain of Okanagan Mountain. From the clay bank benchlands north of Penticton, these craggy, gneiss cliffs are a world turned to stone.

🦌

Legal Description of Property:	Lot A, Plan 24102, District Lot 200 Similkameen Division of Yale Land District
Zoned:	Forestry-Grazing
Everett's description:	50 acres of peripheral, non-agricultural, steep terrain. View lots possible. Residual resource capabilities.
Jay's description:	50 acres of scenic, wild beauty. Limited agricultural development; Natural habitat for protected species. Paradise!
My description:	Vertical rock. Secluded, rugged terrain. 'View' property with challenge. Minimal additional development potential. Bedrock.

🦌

This piece of land constitutes 'real estate,' but the transfer of title represents much more than the exchange of venture capital. The purchase of this property is a legal transaction that fails to convey either the origins or aspirations of those who hold title. The Harrises, who purchased the property in 1968, are a family with a history of living on the land. But neither they nor the previous owner of this parcel were born here; the land was earlier wrested from the territory of First Nations. We are a part of the colonization of this place, another step in the global movement of the human species, our 'settlement' the occupation of a place once home to others. None of this seems to count legally. All that matters is that the title to the land is in the process of changing owners.

The deed to this property confirms our status as 'landed migrants.' Owning land is an induction to a way of life; it will reflect our ability to change, adapt to and survive this place. Whatever game we have been playing is not just about the purchase of land. It's more like an arranged marriage. These negotiations hold our dreams and our future; they dictate relationships, friends and foes; they secure an address, a community and a way of life.

Buying this property takes us well over a year-back and forth on a benchland clay court, surrounded by rocky cliffs. But the rules aren't written down. There is no winner.

We hold title. Holding title means that we can cut trees, subdivide, plant orchards and vineyards, bulldoze hills and move rocks. But do we own the land? Or does the land own us? I wake up in the night riddled with doubt. Maybe this deadpan piece of rock is just a commodity, sold to the biggest fool. It's like buying property on the moon.

But there are days when the air is sweet, the wispy pines bob in the soft wind and the lichen-scabbed cliffs are velveted in leprechaun green. Buying this place is a way of staking a claim, when you are young and rootless and reckless and your life is still before you and you are looking for a place to hang your hat and your heart.

Antelope-brush, *purshia tridentoda,* in bloom.

❦ 3 ❦
Foundations

Okanagan Lake has had a long and complicated prehistorical development... rupture along the Okanagan fault over 50 million years ago; tertiary volcanic and sedimentary activity; regional tectonic forces and stream dissection of an ancient upland; deep erosion from repeated glaciations, and the stagnation and melting of the Fraser Glacier that last occupied the valley 10,000 years ago.

– MURRAY ROED AND JOHN GREENOUGH, GEOLOGY OF THE KELOWNA
AREA AND ORIGIN OF THE OKANAGAN VALLEY OF B.C.

This place is history, a valley scooped by glaciers into its present U-shaped form 10,000 years ago. On the surface, gray-green sage and rabbit-brush crop-share open grasslands of bluebunch wheatgrass, needle and thread grass, red three-awn and fescue, like patchy transplants on a balding pate. Granite cliffs staircase the creek, then surface uphill as a spine of outcrops. At the house site, rock sizzles in a griddle of hardpan. Bedrock borders and defines the property.

Gneisses are often folded and deformed from an earlier plastic state into curves and ripples. All around me, rock is striated in gray and pink or white. Or chunked in big rectangular blocks of monotone pewter. Or flowing smooth and round like Henry Moore sculptures, with big round bums and shoulders. Even when you can't see it, rock oozes just beneath a skin of soil.

            ❧

We've entered a time-and-place warp. We buy the place as a campsite, retirement place and conservation project. Instead we find ourselves captive to the land and the project of building a house. I still have doubts.

"You have a Master's degree, for god's sake," spews Jay, fed up with my uncertainty. "You're probably overqualified for most jobs. The College here is expanding and you have lots of teaching experience. What more do you want?" Jay turns uphill and strides away.

I charge after him. "But I just started my new job. It's not teaching. I'd never be able to find another research job in women's health care." This move could be a throwback to pre-feminist terrain, a Cherry Orchard.

Jay shrugs his shoulders and continues up the path. "You've said yourself that you like doing physical work for a change, and you like the challenge of something totally different. As for feminism, well, you're building a house. You're learning about construction and architecture and building structure – non-traditional work for women."

I bolt ahead, so I can turn around to face him. "Look. I'd never be doing this on my own. This project is your idea, your vision. And jobs will be pretty scarce around here – even at the College. This may fit into your résumé, but it will never be in mine."

His shoulders are hunched up to his neck. "Look, life doesn't have any guarantees, but you're bound to get a job, and besides, it'll be much cheaper to live here. Fifty acres of Okanagan rock is a steal compared to a lot in Vancouver ... What's going on? I thought we wanted to get out of the rat race."

"Yeah, but I was just getting into the rat race."

Gender is still an invisible issue in these parts. Do I see myself as Janie Harris? I suspect that the frontier mythology disguises a return to domesticity. We've already purchased two old wood cook stoves from a farmer in Keremeos. They need a little work, but maybe one day they will look like:

"THE OLD BLACK IRON STOVE"

The black iron stove in our kitchen
It truly was wondrous to see,
Its top was so clean and so polished
Our faces we almost could see

Our lives were all centered 'round it,
We fed it the very best wood
So that mother could do all the cooking
And bake our bread yummy and good.

– MAGDA RICE, OKANAGAN HISTORY

I'm not just fiscally conservative; I have different ideas about our impending move. Burrowing into lunch one day, I badger Jay. "Don't you think that building a house is selfish? Aren't we just indulging our whims?"

Jay laughs with relish. "You're kidding, right? This project gives us a chance first-hand to explore the basic impacts of living on the earth! If more people could dig their own foundations, source their own water, and dispose of their own wastes, people would appreciate their impacts on this planet. "

I sputter, "You think we're doing this as a public service? You must be joking!"

He regroups. "Maybe we're not doing it to become self-sufficient. But this project is educational; it could be a teaching tool."

My partner is a man of conviction. The subsidence of my fear is neither as gradual as glacial melt nor as sudden as the lurch of tectonic plates, but it is sufficient to prompt our move from Vancouver. In fact, it is not Jay's zeal, but the Protestant ethic that overrides my ambivalence. The work of building a house up here far outweighs mundane concerns about the future; anything this hard to do must be worthwhile. This is an exercise in faith.

Blind faith.

❦

In the spring of 1974, we settle into Alex and Jeannie's little barn, store our belongings at Frau Schmidt's in Penticton, and gear up for the construction project. At first, we're only making inroads. Well, pathways – a path to the house site from the parking place, to be exact. Tools of the trade include: one pickaxe, one pry bar, two shovels, one mattock (a heavy duty hoe with a blunt wedge), work gloves, work boots, and two wheelbarrows.

The simple engineering is to dig soil from the uphill side of the slope and pile it downhill, converting the steep pitch to a level surface so that we can walk and carry supplies to the house site. Each morning heart-shaped prints of mule deer are embedded in the unpacked soil.

❦

"WIK-A-WIK-A-WIK-A-WIK-A-WIK-A-WIK-A-WIK!"

I leap from bed, run to the kitchen, grab the pie tins, and trip out the door into the gloom of early dawn. Banging the tins against one another, I hiss, "Scram! Get out of there, you goddamned bird! Beat it!"

There is a flutter of movement at the peak of the roof. "Scat" I spit. "Clink, clank, clank," clatter the cymbals of aluminum tins. I sputter, "PSSSSSTT!! PSSSSSSST!!" The flicker swoops away in undulating waves of flight, its white rump just visible in the morning light. Northern flicker, red-shafted (Colaptes auratus).

The northern flicker is the most common woodpecker in the Okanagan. With a freckled breast, salmon under-wings and a black crescent-shaped bib, this bird scallops the air with short, loping flights: a thing of beauty. But not at 4 a.m.

For the last few weeks a flicker has frequented Alex and Jeannie's "barn" where we live. Flickers search for hollow spots - stumps, dead trees, and buildings-to amplify their sound and to attract mates. This one sounds like it's auditioning for a rock and roll band. Sometimes the bird shuffles around, just under the eaves, before it begins to hammer. Other days it starts up like a machine gun. I've started anticipating its arrival, waking at 3:30, 3:15, 3:00. This bird is playing havoc with my sleep.

"I'm gonna' kill that thing," I mutter as I crawl back into bed. Jay shrugs, turns over, and sinks back to sleep. I lie there twitching.

🦌

Later that day, Jay climbs a ladder to the peak of the barn to dangle a couple of pie plates. "These will work when they catch the light." They do, for a day or two. Then the flicker shifts to the other side of the barn, where the noise is even worse. The tiny building amplifies the sound so that it seems to come from everywhere.

The next morning when the drilling starts, I ease outside, clutching my weapon close to my body, like a cop in a shakedown. I aim it vertically, and the loaded squirt gun delivers its liquid payload. Its four-foot range falls just short of the bird, and the water sprinkles back on my head.

Over the next weeks, the bird becomes more obstinate, hunkering in under the eaves between the twirling pie plates and the house. Roused by my ruckus, Jay attempts to physically remove the flicker by poking a twenty-foot pole up and under the bird. It flaps away.

It's 4 a.m. I put the kettle on for tea.

In late May, the old logging bridge quivers as we cross. Chute Creek is crazed with light, air, sound and movement, a jungled crease of bushes, trees and the detritus of spring floods. It sluices through the cliffs, slashes through steep, dark canyons carved from granite cut blocks, swirls around boulders and descends again. The creek tumbles and carouses around the corner, then skydives twenty-five meters in Chute Creek Falls, thrashing into the turmoil of the pool below.

Waves of sound roll uphill, like the sound of teen-aged boys in souped-up cars, engines rumbling, radios throbbing with the pulse of spring. The falls are in full throttle: amber streams of creek water thunder into the canyon; backwash steams the walls in curtains of morning mist. The dank smell of freshwater permeates the air. Over the thunder of the falls a swoon of sound sinks from a high wail into an earth moan and back again, as if jet aircraft were taking off and landing. The score would look something like this:

THE CHUTE CREEK FALLS OVERTURE

BACKGROUND

Waterfall:	*Whooooosh, rumble, rumble, oohhhnnnnnh*
Kingfisher scoops creek:	*Chatchatchatchatchatchata*

(SHIFT TO FOREGROUND)

Robins:	*Chirp, cheerup, chortle, churrrp*
Northern flicker:	*(Machine gun) Ratatatatatatat*
Waterfall:	*Sluuurrrpppp, whhssh, ohhnnn, onhhh, ssslllppp*
California quail:	*Koocoooya, Cakoooyup, Kakoooya*
Townsend's solitaire:	*Soft one note: Deeeeeeeee*
Chickadees:	*Dee (high) dee dee dee dee dee*

OFFSTAGE

Waterfall:	*Aaaahuunnnn, schlllurrrbb, whiiishshhsh, bubbulabubba, aahhnnh…*

A friend of the Harrises has purchased property on the other side of the creek. Eleanor, who is a potter, sculptor and painter, will be our nearest neighbour. She is tall, spirited and articulate, with a British accent (which seems to come with the territory), and a robust laugh. Her river of auburn hair cascades like the creek, warm and suffused with light and a will of its own. As we hurtle up the road one day we see her at the top of the hill.

"I'll show you my house plans the next time you stop", says Eleanor, as we pull over. She points to a flat stretch just off the logging road, lined by tall cottonwoods. "This used to be an irrigation ditch. It ran from the creek downhill to Graham's property, which is now Harrises. It has enough soil for a garden, and I'll plant additional trees for shade."

Then she sighs. "This is taking much longer than I'd anticipated. I'm still working on the design". Eleanor gestures across the steep hillside. "Not to mention water or power or contractors. They can't imagine that a single woman wants to build a house in the bush."

A few hours later, Eleanor and two younger women appear at our building site. Terri and Meryl introduce themselves. "Eleanor was our teacher at the Kootenay School of Art", says Terri. "We've come to give her a hand. She's always up to something new!"

Eleanor's eyes sparkle. "The girls and I are renting out Hunt's basement while we start on the house. You must stop in."

Jay walks Eleanor around the site, giving her the imaginary house tour around batter boards and lines of string that describe the planned site. It's like the emperor's new clothes. We're hoodwinked by the illusion of living here, imagining we could inhabit this place.

Most of the time, Eleanor is out of sight and sound beyond the chasm and roar of the creek. Our everyday neighbours are the other species who inhabit this place. Today the screech of a red-tailed hawk signals bloodlust, or the mating imperative, or perhaps the ecstasy of wind. A rufous-sided towhee scratches in last year's aspen leaves to scrape up insects; he squawks, something between the scold of a squirrel and the taunt of a jay. In the background, a percussion unit builds from a drone of buzzes and trills to the tapping sounds of a nuthatch, sapsucker or downy woodpecker.

A robin explodes from a juniper bush. Its nest is wedged into a juncture of straggly branches, so deeply embedded that I can barely glimpse the tarn of its egg. I watch the bird as she fluffs her feathers and snuggles down on the nest until only head and tail protrude. Two weeks later, when the eggs hatch, each pulsing little body sac is covered with a fine, light gray down, transformed by the arrival of food into clamoring, open beaks.

Our nesting proceeds more slowly. The first construction project is the outhouse, which boasts a vent, a sloping roof, a pink, second-hand plastic seat, and a door that sags open, facing down the path.

❦

Victor Wilson, who lives with his wife Kitty downhill at Indian Rock, knows the lay of the land better than most anyone else. When we visit to ask advice about the layout of the house, Victor summarizes the Wilson approach: "Kitchens face north and away from the heat, living areas to the south; the house faces down the lake to optimize sun exposure" he clips, with authority and precision. "Flat overhangs deflect the summer sun." As he speaks, Victor's blue-green eyes scale the landscape like a climber looking for new routes, scrambling the rugged contours of Okanagan Mountain.

Victor's ideas coalesce with our own. The new house will be a pre-fabricated log cabin, supplied by our Norwegian friend Bjorn's company, Tru-Craft, easy to assemble and fitting its location in 'the bush.' The Clivus Multrum toilet, a composting waste disposal unit, ordains the basic struc-ture. Kitchen compost will drop into a chute next to the bathroom; in the basement, a huge container will absorb both kitchen and human wastes, consolidating them into one. At least that's what the brochures say.

Today, the nice young couple from Naramata is taking a lunch break from working on the path. "Do you really think the Clivus will com-post?" she muses. "I bet you'll have to stir it up."

He shrugs, his mouth tacky with peanut butter and jam. "Yeah, it'll work..." He grins. " Besides, I've always been a shit disturber."

"But it will smell, don't you think? I mean, even with the fan." She's not convinced. "Just a generation ago, people were getting indoor flush toilets. Do you think this is progress?"

"It's just a very different concept." He is convinced.

He draws the unit for her in the air. "It's got a stack, and a fan, which will create a constant upward draft. All the smells will be funneled out of the house. It won't smell at all." He turns to her as if admonishing a child. "Remember, we're doing this to conserve water. No flushing. And no septic field."

She agrees with him in principle, thinking that if you did a perc test on this site, liquid would bounce back and hit you in the face. "But it's going to look pretty disgusting."

He shrugs. "Yeah, you're right. On the other hand, the toilet will be a great judge of character. Imagine our first dinner party, when people have to use the 'facilities.'"

"I don't think this is a dinner party kind of place."

🐦

Dear Nancy and Pierre:

To get to the house site, drive north out of town, and stay straight on the main road. Keep left at the "Y" turnoff to Chute Lake, go downhill over a cattle guard, and take a right on the next unmarked road. After bumping along for a few hundred metres, gun the car uphill, and hold on! After the Chilkoot Trail section, the road crosses Chute Creek on an old logging bridge. Curve up a steep sandy slope, then park next to our yellow truck. Follow the path to a rocky, bare plateau overlooking the lake. See you soon!

P.S. If you get lost, just stop and ask for directions. Everybody knows us.

🐦

We have become a pilgrimage. Vancouver friends come for the weekend to bludgeon boulders into submission or carry building materials out to the building site. Tired of the same old drag? Come for the weekend, limber up, get some exercise in the fresh clean Okanagan air!

And they do! Audrey schleps dimensional lumber down the path. David and Lynette and their daughter Ainsley carry supplies. Bev and Eve haul loads in the tractor. The day after Pierre and Nancy's visit, Jay throws down the pickaxe and wipes his dusty face with his shirtsleeve. "I've got it. We could go commercial and put an ad in the Globe. People would pay for therapy. I can see it now...

* * * * * * * * * * * * * *

Tune into nature. Get in touch with your body.
Spend a week at The Granite Farm. Clean air.
Good exercise. An organic experience!

* * * * * * * * * * * * * *

"We could charge thousands. Get all those stressed out business guys on Bay Street to come and push wheelbarrow loads of dirt. They'd get their money's worth!"

❦

The South Okanagan's warm, arid climate and mountainous topography make it home to many species that do not exist elsewhere in Canada. The next time we stop in at Harrises to visit, Janie meets us at the front porch, and motions us in, wiping her hands on a towel. "Have you heard about the woodpecker?" she asks. The kitchen window overlooks the old barn and a yard full of rusted-out machinery.

"What woodpecker?" asks Jay. About twenty feet up the air, a feeder hangs from the branch of an enormous fir tree, spinning.

Janie nods to us in a conspiratorial fashion. "A white-headed woodpecker!" She's whispering, as if reporters were hidden under the kitchen table, as if it's a pterodactyl or a flying woolly mammoth or a copper-tailed trogon. I forget that we're living in a Museum of Natural History.

"I didn't think there were any white-headed woodpeckers this far north," says Jay, his voice raised, his eyes glued to the feeder. "How long has it been coming? Is there a breeding pair? When do they come to the feeder?

Janie brushes her hair out of her eyes. " A Japanese photographer has been here the last two days. He's managed to get a few shots. I can't remember ever seeing them before."

Picoides albolarvatus: White head and throat. Male: red patch on back of head, black body, white wing patches. Nests in coniferous mountain forests, especially ponderosa; feeds on seeds from pinecones, and harvests insects and larvae beneath loose bark. Zygodactyl feet, with two toes forward and two back, support clinging to vertical surfaces. Woodpeckers make noise in the process of excavation, foraging and drumming.

Homo sapiens north naramatensis: Inhabits marginal land. Semi-vertical posture; erratic and inefficient foraging patterns. Strongly marked plumage in both male and female-with red jacket diagnostic of female in winter months. Activity during prolonged excavation and nesting periods includes aggressive posturing and varied verbal calls. This species adapts well to piciformes activities, providing potential feeding sites, excellent drumming soundboards and nesting habitat. Also highly territorial.

Spring melts into summer. Every day there's a new act in the open-air theatre of our work site. In early May, tiny knots of translucent, golden-green aspen leaves open to the sun. Wildflowers unfurl across the plateau, rappel rocky bluffs and cliffhang steep clefts, fearless of heights. Some of these spring blossoms are unique to the dry Interior.

I look up their Latin names to recognize their unique characteristics. At our feet, golden stamens of shooting star (*Dodecatheon pulchellum*) dart through magenta petals. Creamy death camas (*Zigadenus venenosus*) sprinkles the house site; butter-curled oregon grape (*Mahonia aquifolium*) is ready to bloom at the parking site. Fragile ferns (*Cystopteris fragilis*) fiddlehead from rocky crevices. Each day greets us with:

MORE FLOWERS OF THE GRANITE FARM:

Fringe-cup	*Lithophragma parviflorum*
Larkspur	*Delphinium nuttallianum*
Yellow Bells	*Fritillaria pudica*
Snow Buckwheat	*Eriogonum niveum*
Lemonweed	*Lithospermum ruderale*
Penstemon	*Penstemon fruticosus*
Chocolate lily	*Fritillaria lanceolata*
Bitterroot or rock rose	*Lewisia rediviva*
Thread-leaved Phacelia	*Phacelia linearis*
Chocolate Biscuitroot	*Lomatium dissectum*
Desert Parsley	*Lomatium macrocarpum*
Stonecrop	*Sedum lanceolatum*
Pussytoes	*Antennaria dimorpha*
Yarrow	*Achillea millefolium*

Blossoms soften the rocky soil, racing the summer's heat, but through this fluorescence we are preoccupied with digging. We don't sing the chorus. We're just learning the words.

🦌

Scotty, the contractor who is building Alex and Jeannie's house, has taken a shine to us. He thinks we're crazy to build the house this far from the main road. Today he walks around the dig, and nods towards the lake.

"For the last time, build the bloody house where you'll get the best view! You're daft to be building it here anyway."

"But Scotty," I reply, "It's supposed to blend in with its surroundings. We don't want people to see the house. It's going to be unobtrusive."

He wrinkles his nose, narrows his eyes, and pushes his hat back further on his balding head. "It sure as hell will be! Who would ever look up here anyway? And why for the love of God would you want it to blend with this?" He motions uphill, to the scabby rockfall hillside.

Silence. Jay looks down the lake, and I fuss with my boots. Scotty shakes his head in disbelief and then takes a deep breath. "You'd be done the thing in a wink of time if you set it down below, where you can get your supplies. Power. Phone."

He shrugs, turns and strides back up the path to his truck.

❦

The warmth of spring may bring a prickle at the back of the neck. If you are quick enough, you can grip it between your thumb and forefinger and pull it out of your hair before it self-installs. I abhor wood ticks. They not only carry tick paralysis; their simple blood thirst makes them repugnant. They want you, in a B-grade horror film vampire way. They need you.

Sometimes they hitch a ride up your clothes. Female ticks have a white mark on their backs, which stands out just enough to make them visible. You're brushing your hair when suddenly you feel a tiny lump.

"Jay, come quick!" I'm leaning over the bathroom sink, twisting towards the bare light bulb, grabbing at my hair.

He runs into the bathroom, where I'm straining to see the back of my head in the mirror. "I think it's another tick. But I don't want the trial by fire, like last time."

"It worked, didn't it? I blew out the match, and placed it against the tick, and it backed right out of there. It was easy, and it didn't hurt. "

"O.K., it worked. But I didn't like the smoke coming out of my hair."

I straddle the bathtub rim. Jay peers down at my scalp. "Yup, you've got another one. I never seem to get any. Maybe it's because you have longer hair."

"I don't care. Just get it out of there. Fast."

"We have to be careful," he says. "If we don't get the head of the tick out, it will fester."

Jay should be an Emergency Response Technician. He's quick and calm and steady with his hands. "Why don't we try the oil method I read about?" he says, thinking out loud. "What can we use?" He opens up the medicine chest. "How about baby oil?"

"O.K. it's there on the top shelf. What's that supposed to do?"

"It's supposed to smother the tick. It will back out and I'll grab it, like the last one. O.K. now, hold still." He dips a Q-tip in the baby oil, and smears it around the tick, where the head is attached.

"There, he's starting to move, and I'll just help him a bit, like this ..." He pulls the tick out with the tweezers and searches for a guillotine knife.

"Now that's one nervous tic."

Excavation: First Stage. Excavating this site takes us all summer. Shovels shudder and scrape into underlying rock; pickaxes, pry bars and mattocks bite into dry earth. By June, the heat is suffocating. We are not shoveling and carting dirt-we are picking through rock field. The old loop-the-loop swing, from pay dirt piles of earth, then over the shoulder and into the wheelbarrow, the one where you can get a rhythm going? That doesn't happen much.

Instead, you strike at rock, rock thinly camouflaged as soil, rock with roots, rock, that if it had its druthers, wouldn't be going anywhere. The reverberations of each bad swing, each rock shock, shoot up your arm and down your back and into your hand, like a palsy. You go after each reluctant rock with a pry bar, angling every which way, until you slowly wedge it out of its niche. When you do get a clump of small rocks puffed by silty soil, you try to slide the shovel underneath, through a gravelly groan of resistance, until you get a loving spoonful. Then you heave it up and into the wheelbarrow. The pulverized dirt sifts into your lungs.

The larger excavation at this site is geophysical. Ten thousand years ago, when this valley was glaciated, Lake Penticton was ice-dammed near Okanagan Falls, pooling deeper and larger than today's 140-kilometer long Okanagan Lake. Its basin captured the sediments that form the silt bluffs and benchlands that support orchards and vineyards today.

Far above the lakebed, the rock at the house site is crusted with cryptogamic soil, made up of algae and lichens-fairylands of elemental growth. Ear against the ground, as if I'm divining oceans from a conch shell, I imagine the groans of glaciers in retreat. In early June, tiny clusters of rockrose wave their tentacles like dryland sea anemones. In summer this arid land becomes an ocean of heat.

Since glacial times this house site has been frequented by a succession of others. In just a few months we've seen coyotes and mule deer, elk, rabbits, marmots, and grouse and owls. First Nations pictographs, like the 'Indian Rock' now perched above the Naramata Road and the pelican drawing at Paradise Ranch, mark an indigenous presence long after the retreat of glaciers.

How will our brief tenure be inscribed on this place?

Bitterroot, *Lewisia rediviva.*

❦ 4 ❦
Habitat

It is hard to describe the degrading influence, which thinning & picking fruit has on one
... instead of delicately snipping with precision & care, I felt more inclined to tear off the
measly little apples, or to take an axe and cut the trees to bits ... I muttered profanities
against all manner of fruit & fruit-growers ...

— JOHN SUGARS. AN OKANAGAN HISTORY: THE DIARIES
OF ROGER JOHN SUGARS 1905-1919

Fruit trees surround the little barn where we live, but we're oblivious to their variety, maintenance and harvest. At the end of June, white pits of new cherries have swollen to hues of salmon pink and ripened through the Revlon spectrum from persimmon and strawberry red into hues of cranberry and deeper burgundy. Driving along the road into town, cherry orchards are beginning to look a lot like Christmas.

The Okanagan valley swells into spring with the telltale signs of a tree fruit economy. Although grapes and urban development have begun to encroach, tree fruits occupy about three quarters of the 1970's land base, comprising the main agricultural industry. On the road into Penticton, guys wear doomsday respirators as they perch on tractors pulling tanks of spray. Co-op trucks cart faded racks of red bins to the packinghouse. At the foot of driveways along the Naramata Road, the latest crop of pickers throng beneath ripened fruit.

One day Alex trudges up the driveway, heading towards his upper cherry block, hands in pockets, slumping. Things could be better. He's having a hard time finding pickers. With a small acreage, it's difficult to get people for the different harvests. The cherries are almost ready to go, but it's been looking like more rain. Soon the crop will be shot.

🦌

Our first day as pickers, we meet Alex at seven in the morning. He sets up ladders and buckets. The ladders are three-legged - two supporting the steps, but only a post, like a pivot, propping up the other side. The rungs aren't flat, but rounded. No grip. By 4:00, I'm exhausted. My arms and legs and shirt and shorts are covered with cherry juice, like shrapnel wounds. My hands are stained purple, even under my finger-nails.

Jay and I climb down our ladders. Maybe we're being too picky.

Alex lopes downhill to check on our progress. He takes one look at our buckets, then glances at our buckets of seconds, and shakes his head, "Well, what's this?"

I chirp. "Those are our seconds. You told us not to pick splits or bruised ones, but we can use them ourselves."

Alex sighs. "I don't think you understand. This is a business! I have to get this fruit to market."

He scans the two trees and the seconds buckets, shaking his head. "At this rate, my cherries will get to the co-op three weeks later than anyone else's, split from rain and delay. It's too late." He turns and walks away, calling over his shoulder "Tomorrow just try to pick. Don't think. Just pick."

🦌

Forecast for the south Okanagan valley and Southern Interior, British Columbia. June 23, temperatures cooler than normal. Winds from the southeast, 25 gusting to 40. Likelihood of precipitation 40%. Increasing to 60% tomorrow.

As we walk through the cherry block the next day, I notice movement higher up in the branches. A couple of Quebecois pickers have parked their van up the road. The bottom of their bin is already covered in cherries.

"Bonjour, les copains," I smile as we walk up to them.

"Salût les deux," beams a face above us in the leaves.

"Vous avez cuelli combien de paniers hier?" I ask her.

"Ummh. Qu'est ce que tu crois, Claude?" she looks over to a long-haired guy on the top rung of a ladder at the next tree. As if he's just hit the jackpot, or pulled three cherries on the slots, fruit tumbles into his bucket. "Moi, je ne compte pas. C'est plus façile comme ca."

Claude descends from the clouds of greenery, grinning. "Mais hier j'ai cuelli d'environs 50 paniers. Et vous autres?"

Jay walks up the road in disgust, shaking his head. "We got 10 each!"

We bring the radio with us to listen to CBC. We're starting to get the hang of picking. We drink twice as much tea and take fewer breaks. We try to be more ruthless and to discard bruised fruit. My neck and shoulders are killing me, but on Saturday, our last day, together we fill 35 buckets!

Alex sidles up to us with a rueful smile, " I don't know just how to say this. But you're the slowest pickers I've ever seen."

🐌

Excavation: Second Stage. It's too hot to work outdoors in the midsummer Okanagan unless you wake up before dawn. We roast through day after day of relentless sun, with no shade. By the end of each day we're filthy and exhausted. The locals have it figured out: start work before dawn, finish by early afternoon and then go to the beach.

🐌

Excavation: Third Stage. A blanket of heat seeps down the parched July hillsides. It's over 30 degrees in the shade, except that there isn't any. Before the barrow is full I wheel another load up the path and over to the crumbling rocky hillside that could some day be a garden, except it's so hot nothing could grow there but cactus. The cross-strut on the front of the wheelbarrow stops me dead in my tracks if I carry the load at too acute an angle, so I nudge the wheelbarrow along in an almost horizontal position, lifting it with my forearms, keeping the angle low. As I teeter up the path, sweat drips down my forehead and puddles into dust at my neck. I can barely move in this sledgehammer heat.

The glacial origins of this valley are mythology.

🐌

I'm fed up with digging, with Jay, and especially with my own compliance in this project. Why would anyone build a house in such a rocky, untenable spot? I'm hallucinating in the heat. Perhaps "others" out here are engaged in their own domestic negotiations. Just imagine:

"Hey SSSsssssssibyl," Randy whispers, slithering his ropy reptilian form towards her.

"Don't 'hey' me, Randy. "Enough sweet talk." Sibyl's olive-brown form slides towards the light. "You know, fall is coming on, and we haven't even started looking for a new den.

"A new hibernaculum?" he spits. "But this one's tested and true!"

She's having none of it. "You tried to pull the same stunt last year. Promised me everything, spring and summer, with all those eggs hatching and these new predators nosing about. Now they're here every day."

Her tongue darts in and out as she slides towards the crevice opening and extends her spade-shaped head. "Look! They're denning on our property! Right out in the open. It's hotter than hell out there! Homo sapiens? Just what are they thinking?" she hisses in disgust.

The Western Rattlesnake (Crotalus viridis) is one of British Columbia's largest snakes; Most rattlesnakes live out their lives near a winter den (hibernaculum) and return faithfully to it each autumn...snakes are vulnerable to human-caused disturbance and killing ... they prefer dry, usually rocky and rugged landscapes with sparse or scattered tree cover. Terrain having suitable hibernating sites is important for rattlesnakes. In British Columbia this usually involves rocky ridges with crevices or deep talus slopes.

—WESTERN RATTLESNAKE, WILDLIFE IN BRITISH COLUMBIA AT RISK.
PROVINCE OF BRITISH COLUMBIA, MINISTRY OF ENVIRONMENT,
LANDS AND PARKS.

Sibyl curls back towards Randy. "Soon as you can shake it, we'll be history. They have a thing about snakes."

He rasps, "Remember the story? About the guys who came up from the ranch and shot out our Little Diamondback cousins on the lower east side of the cliff?"

She swooshes him back. "That's not as bad as the time they torched the whole family on the northern talus perimeter. Grandpa was out of the den when it happened. All he heard was footsteps, the clink of metal and that horrible smell. They poured the stuff out of the can and a spark seared right into the rock, back to Grandma and all the young ones. Meltdown!"

Randy sidles up to Sibyl. "You're right. We've got to get out of this place!"

In August, we become the proud parents of a juvenile flying squirrel, retrieved by Leslie and Stuart's dog from some unknown place. We heat milk and feed him day and night with a dropper. Lindy is nocturnal; he comes to life in the evening, when we take him out of his bird cage and watch him scrabble around the room, around the bed, across the kitchen counter, up the drapes, across the kitchen floor. As we lie reading in bed, he darts over and under our pajamas-an erratic movement with scratchy claw marks, up and down.

We start wearing underwear to bed.

                                          ❦

"We can't keep him, you know," I blurt to Jay at about 2:30 in the morning. "Lindy's got to live where he can be a squirrel."

"Mmph." Jay's head is burrowed under the pillow. "He's a squirrel here."

"Yeah, but what about wild life? We're moving here so that we get to see things in the wild, not in our living room."

I'm talking to a pillow. "And there's also the nocturnal thing." I listen to scratching sounds as Lindy scampers down the counters and across the floor.

"You're nocturnal anyway. Maybe you should take the night shift." Jay turns over and is immediately asleep.

                                          ❦

Excavation: Last Stage. During the day, we dig. The deeper we dig, the more the house can nestle into the site. But we run into rock at the north end of the excavation. In the corner basement bedroom, the floor will be like mountains rising from the plains. It's August, late in the afternoon. The sun has been suspended forever above Summerland. We're slowing down, losing momentum.

"What about dynamite?" asks our friend Robbie, standing at the rim of the house site. Robbie's one of those guys who gets things done fast, who doesn't spend a lot of time talking. He wrote his Master's thesis in a week. "That way you could speed things up a bit."

"Yeah, but dynamite's hard to control," says Jay, squinting up at Robbie and leaning on the pickaxe, while he catches his breath. "What if we blew the place up? It would look like a mine site. Or worse, a crater. Or a quarry."

"I hate to be the one to break it to you," Robbie grins. "But it wouldn't matter much. It's all rock anyway. It wouldn't look much different."

He turns and walks away, stops, and calls over his shoulder: "And if it goes wrong, you could fix it up with a garden, like they did with Queen Elizabeth Park in Vancouver, or what's it called, Butcher's Gardens over there on the Island. It'd save you a month of digging, that's all."

Western Rattlesnake, *Crotalus viridis.*

❦ 5 ❦
Footprints

Home ... is more than a sense of belonging. It's all the various ways we fit ourselves into a landscape, meet its demands, give it a human significance ... The exterior landscapes become internal necessities.

— JUDITH KITCHEN, WHEN WE SAY WE'RE HOME

Excavating means carving out, defining and leveling the site, cultivating the space for the foundations of a home. The foundations include the footings, the slab and the walls of cinder blocks on which the rest of the house will be built.

Footings are the feet of the house, the concrete around the perimeter that connects soil and rock with the building that will someday stand in this place. Footings will link this glacial-scoured, lichen-blotted rock and its thin accumulation of soil cover to a building — logs and windows and porches and stairs — and the humans who inhabit it.

Getting your footing means gaining confidence, learning to feel comfortable in a place. Footing is gerund, both noun and verb for how you experience a place through your feet, placing one foot in front of the other, one step at a time.

To foot it is the infinitive. We have walked, climbed, ambled, strolled, hoofed and hiked almost every niche of this acreage. Our feet weave a crisscross of routes, as if the act of walking stitches the landscape into one single fabric.

The footprint of the house is the weight of its impact on the earth, including the materials used as well as the ecological consequences of building and living here.

Reverend Beale and his wife have moved from Naramata into the Retirement Centre in Penticton. Tucked behind the packinghouse, their lakeside cabin looks north to Peachland. Okanagan Lake is a different body of water in the fall, a sea whose northerlies pound the shore, rattle the window frames and seethe through the walls. We bundle inside for the winter.

Lindy's move is a bigger problem. He's getting more and more squirrelly in the house, but we don't know how to help him adjust to living in the wild. Jay builds a small box, just bigger than a birdhouse, and cushions the inside of the box with strips of old flannel and a big red woolen sock. He nails it to the big Douglas fir next to the parking lot at our new house site. We'll bring Lindy food and water, and check in on him every day. There will be enough human activity in the vicinity for him to be weaned gradually from our presence.

That afternoon, when we introduce him to his new home, he buries himself in the box, sticks his head out through the round front hole, and then digs back inside to nest. The next day we drive to the house site early, but there is no trace of the squirrel. The only sign is the red sock, pulled out partially through the entry hole.

"How could we have been so stupid?" Jay slumps against the tree. "We should have trained him — how to hide, what to eat. How could something have found him so quickly?

He sinks to the ground, mumbling. "It must have been a ferret, or an owl. Why did we ever adopt him? How can you possibly keep something so wild? What were we thinking?"

Jay doesn't talk to anyone for a week.

❦

We're not the only ones behind schedule. One afternoon, we stop to visit Eleanor, who gestures hopelessly at the forms for the foundations to her house, old weather-beaten boards barely tacked together. "Sometimes I doubt I shall ever have a house," she laments. In the afternoon light, her hair reflects the soft ruddy hues of ponderosa pine.

"Well Eleanor, we are in the bush. And, this is the Okanagan." I'm trying to cajole her.

She barks back. "I know this is the Okanagan! I was born and raised here!"

❦

"Sometimes it feels like we're extras in a Monty Python movie," I mention to Jay one night in our wee cottage on the lake. "Why are so many of our neighbours British? Here the sun still seems to be setting on the British empire. Alex was born in Pakistan, Harrises are from Africa, Eleanor's parents were British, as were Wilson's. They all have a stiff upper lip, a formality topped with endless endurance and optimism."

He considers this, "It seems to be a generational thing." Then he adds, "But it must be more than coincidence. Maybe it's the legacy of 'remittance men', sons of wealthy families, sent abroad and supported on family stipends..."

I interrupt, "Or maybe the Okanagan is a renaissance kind of place. Just think, a hundred years ago cattle munched these grasslands. By the turn of the century there were paddle wheelers and the CPR, then orchards and the Kettle Valley Railway. Now it's tourism and urbanization. And grapes." I try to imagine my aunt moving here just forty years ago.

JOURNAL ENTRY: BEATRICE ARUNDEL HOWE, SEPTEMBER 17, 1934

The day begins with a brisk northwesterly, which interrupts boat service from Summerland. My sister Marguerite is due any day now from England. In the meantime, I have kept busy in anticipation, harvesting the crops and preparing for my second winter in this bleak but bountiful land.

Following our disappointment with the boat, the children and I return to Arawana Ranch. We enjoy a tasty treat of leftovers from yesterday's tea, and resume the harvest. With fruit ripening on the vine there is no respite. I've set the children to pulling up carrots, rutabagas, onions and potatoes for the root cellar. Later, while they are busy with their studies, I will continue putting the garden to bed. Then I'll feed the animals and begin dinner.

Oliver returns home at dusk, following a hard day planting new fruit trees and cutting shingles for the new house. With a little luck, we should be able to move in before winter. I am looking forward to having a real roof overhead after months of makeshift frame tent living. The new baby is expected in about four months, so I will have much to prepare before then.

More truckloads of supplies are due before the snow comes – cinder blocks, lumber and shingles for the roof. Truck drivers balk at carrying their loads up the steep hill. They can't believe that anybody's crazy enough to build a house up here. Each load requires a suspension of their disbelief.

We buy a yellow Mazda rotary-engine mini-truck with enough power to horse its way up the hill in the winter and carry loads like the logs and trusses.

By October, the descent of early evenings shortcuts the afternoons. We've spent the best part of the year. We're left with the loose change.

❦

October 15. The Clivus Multrum toilet has arrived! It's made of a mottled German chocolate fiberglass, with a blue trap door at the bottom for removing finished 'waste products.' Scratched into its fibreglass shell is '#3,"-the third unit imported into Canada. It's about eight feet long, and five feet high-a tank-shaped sledge with a flat roof, a roundish bottom and a topside with a few small openings. Tilted on end in the basement, human and food wastes will slump, consolidate, and compost to a final mixture at the bottom.

In this rocky wasteland, the disposal of human wastes presents a special problem. "Waste disposal" seems redundant-getting rid of something you've already eliminated. "Wasting away." "Getting wasted." To waste someone is to eliminate them. Waste is a pejorative.

The word has moral overtones in a culture that denies elimination. Human wastes are the vector of disease; they signal a lack of control. "Scare the piss out of me," pissant, piss-poor, or bullshit, horseshit, you can't "take the shit," you're "full of shit... the list goes on. The potential utility of human wastes is ignored: we are intent in diverting it, covering it up or pretending that it just doesn't happen.

❦

Jay has framed all the footings and the pad for the basement. By late October, two-by-fours are propped up vertically at eight-foot intervals. Inside this perimeter, the pour site is scraped level and cat-cradled by lines of string. The polyethylene pipe from the creek is rigged. Humps of sand and gravel are piled on the north side of the open pit. We're almost ready to pour concrete.

Scotty stops by one afternoon to check the angles and positioning of batterboards. He dangles the plumb line. "Yessirree, that should do her. You'll want to get going pretty soon. Winter's coming on and it won't get any easier."

Across the lake, the snow descends to just above Summerland.

🦌

Victor Wilson has loaned us a gas-powered concrete mixer. This is the first time we've had powered machinery on site. Although we're not Luddites, the house site is a long way from the road, and the road is a long way from a source of power.

We get out to the site early. Robbie and Joanne have come up to help us out. Jay cranks up the generator, and the noise surges up and down, sounding like the birth of the industrial revolution. "uh huh uh huh uh Huhuh Huhuhu Huhuh HUHHUH HUHHUH uhuhuh."

Then we start up the portable cement mixer, and the cement and water slurp into the small rotating tank. "Clank, clank, clank, sluurrrpp, schlooorrp, rattle rattle, CLANK, CLANK, SLURP."

The little cylinder cranks around erratically, chugging like a ratchety locomotive, the slurry slopping up and over the sides. Jay adds cement, testing the texture like a cake mix, and dribbles in a bit more water. The thing snorts and shudders, coughs and screeches.

"KABOOM!!!!"

A thunderclap of sound reverberates in the stillness. A plastic/metallic smell, like a road accident, seeps into the air, accompanied by a cloud of smoke. Then silence. I lift my head to look for the others. Joanne crawls out from behind the small pile of gravel as Jay sidles back into sight from behind the big fir tree. I've run up the path and around the corner. Robbie is halfway to Kelowna.

When the dust settles and our hearts have stopped pounding, we straggle back to the mixer.

Robbie's the first one back. "What the hell happened?"

Jay is closing in on the smoking machine. "It exploded! The damned thing blew up!"

Robbie raises his eyebrows. "But what happened to it? It was like an attack, man. The attack of the killer cement mixer."

Jay is gingerly poking at the steaming bits of crusty, rusty machinery. "It was already pretty old. It's shot. How can we explain this to Victor?"

The smell of singed wire sears the clear cold day.

Load after load of concrete churns in the barrel of the new, rented mixer. We tamp it down into the forms along the house perimeter, and then pour the slab, a 12-by-20 foot section a day. Once it's set, Jay perches on the tacky floor like a water glider. The blade of the concrete finisher surfaces and polishes the surface until it's smooth as a skating rink.

A five hundred gallon storage tank will store gray water from the sinks and shower. A pill-shaped cylinder with vertical ends, the holding tank looks like a miniature submarine. It's too big for the tractor cart, so we skid it out on the frozen path, using a block and tackle and creative language. Above the steep downhill descent of the hillside, the Clivus looks like an armoured personnel carrier.

Breathing heavily, Jay spouts, "Don't you see? We won't have to flush! We won't run into problems when the pipes freeze, or there's not enough water in the creek."

I am beginning to understand the dynamics of waste disposal. I grumble: "What it means, is that we're going to be living with our own shit! Even animals remove their own waste from their living space. Who knows whether or not it will work."

Jay is ahead of his time. "We're being innovative here, trying something new, and this is the perfect place to do it. This is a proven technology." He sighs, "We've built the whole bloody house around this. Why
are you getting cold feet now?"

"Because it's already November?" But maybe it's because I'm finally
seeing the technology. It's primitive. It reminds me of those ironclad
boats in the American civil war, the Merrimac and the Monitor.

I do not say: "This fiberglass bin looks like it was manufactured in a
third grade classroom. Alternative technology makes sense in theory,
but this toilet is just an in-house outhouse."

Jay listens to my silence. Then he shrugs, puts his shoulder to the
Merrimac, and pushes.

My internal dialogue goes something like this: Would I be building this
house by myself? No. It is not my project. It is ours. "We" assumes common objectives – working together in a cooperative endeavor. But this
mutual objective also assumes an equality that is fictional. What each of
us brings to this project, learns and gains from it when we're done is not
the same. Jay has learned this curriculum throughout his life; this project
in turn contributes to his skills.

What am I doing here?

Building a house requires physical strength, technology, and specific knowledge sets. We're constructing not only a house, but also a
marriage; our relationship is both material and emotional. Working together every day on a project in which we have unequal skills gives us
something in common, but puts additional stress on the relationship.
We have learned how to "parallel task", but we rarely agree about what
to do and how to do it.

You never hear about 'remittance women.'

❦

By mid-November, the house site contains:
- 1 x 2's, 2 x 4's, 2 x 3's, 2 x 6's, 2 x 8's, 2 x 10's, and 4 x 4's;
- Sand, gravel, cement, insulation, concrete blocks, rebar;
- Ladders, picks and shovels;
- Logs and wavy-edged siding;
- Clivus Multrum container, gray water tank;
- Roofing shingles for the roof, nails, screws, and other hardware – joist hangers, finishing nails, gyprock nails, spikes, screws and nails of every type and size;
- Windows and doors;
- Sheets of plywood;
- The first dusting of snow.

❦

I'm getting the hang of cinder blocks now, laying the mortar base thick enough, keeping the blocks level, and overlapping the layers as they rise. They form industrial, bad-side-of-town walls, as if a prison has been drilled into this field of golden grass.

Jay frames the basement doorway, adds a plank, and, for the first time, you can walk through a portal into something that could become a house. We stand inside and look at the concrete blocks along the back wall. From here it looks like a warehouse, with a ten-foot clearance for the composting unit. A log house on top of these walls will look like a high-rise Hudson's Bay fort.

The walls distinguish what is inside from what is outside. Snakes and bears and wavy grasses and crooked firs, thorn-slivered paddles of cactus and puffball pine trees are outside.

Only humans could live inside a place like this.

❦

It's late November. I'm out at the site, digging and stacking and organizing the materials. Everything is gray - rock, bushes, trees, the air, the hole in the ground, me. The sky is muffled, as if someone has closed the lid. I'm going through the motions of an exercise disconnected from the rest of the world. A slow agony of doubt descends over me; I can't hold it back. This is different from my occasional frustration at Jay or impatience at our lack of progress. This is the slow quicksand pall of knowing that I am truly stuck. The spell of neighborhood and work and progress has dribbled away. I miss my work and friends. I've lost the opportunity to ruminate and conduct research, to conceptualize for a living.

How could I throw that all away?

Chute Creek.

❦ 6 ❦
Contracting Out

...Even though the house isn't finished, we know we've already moved the important things. We've moved the desire, and the hope, and what we imagine for our futures. This, now, is the place we mean when we speak the word home. This is our home. Our desire.

— WHEN WE SAY WE'RE HOME: A QUARTET OF PLACE
AND MEMORY, W. SCOTT OLSEN

We've hired help.

With his transit set on a barber shop-flagged tripod, Scotty barks out commands to his helper Andy, and Jay. The recipe for framing is in Scotty's head. He measures and figures and levels and squares, right now plotting where the windows are going to go and calculating how to frame up and around them. He grabs the blueprints, yanks a pencil from his paint-splotched carpenter's vest, and scribbles on the horizontal two-by-six, yelling at Jay: "Let's get this run up here. Just get those in, down the way, and she'll have enough strength to stand on her own."

Jay frenetically swings his hammer, trying to toenail the nails, to drive them at a diagonal. Scotty rips more two-by-sixes to size, his pencil stuck behind his ear, his blue eyes sizing up the puzzle. I run back and forth between Scotty and Jay as if I'm in a silent movie with everything jerking and ratcheted up. Scotty swears at nobody in particular. He must have miscalculated another length; the saw squeals again.

❦

Tonight we're having canned soup for dinner. It's dark and the waves slap the shore just outside our little house.

"Did it ever occur to you that although we're living in the Interior, we're outdoors most of the time?" I'm musing out loud. "Except for ashrams in the Kootenays, most of the soul-searching seems to be coastal, like Cold Mountain, or the Esalen Institute."

I'm looking north from our little house/boat up the lake, where our building site is swallowed by bumpy, granite hills. I continue: "We could write The Zen of Cinderblock. From now on, let's say that we've moved to the Exterior..."

Jay joins in. "And found bliss, fulfillment," he grins. "Enlightenment."

I look out into the dark night. "Endarkenment."

❦

When is a roof a floor? When it's the roof of the basement, the subfloor.

The foundations of this house now include: the excavation; basement slab; footings; cinder blocks filled with concrete to grade (soil level); and now, framing to subfloor.

While I cart dimensional lumber and plywood from the parking lot, Scotty and his crew work full tilt Andy lays out the joists, two-by-eights on end crossing the entire width of the house. A fretwork of horizontal lines splice the horizontal walls like the exoskeleton of an enormous, stolid insect.

❦

By mid-December, the "build/ing," this house in the process of being built, is fresh and clean; it smells like a Christmas tree lot. The dank smell of concrete has been replaced by the clean scent of freshly cut wood. There is snow on the ground, and the air is crisp as the circular saw spins excess chunks of wood into the air, reducing linear board feet to pencil sharpenings. Sawdust streamers scatter the slab, curlicues of fir in Shirley Temple curls. .

Soft and pliable and sweet.

If it were not for texture and smell, you would have a hard time linking these materials to a source. This pile of wood is a still life. Trees composed of cellulose and sap, insects and leaves, shade and nests and cover and habitat have been scaled to dimensional lumber – a two-by-four, by-six, by-eight; timber cut to human scale – hundreds of feet of cedar or fir reduced to uniform lengths, graded according to strength and type of wood and bearing capacity.

The two-by-sixes used for bearing walls are B.C. fir, from the Chilcotin, the Sunshine Coast or the Island: a luscious buttery-beige, damp from being stacked together and the melt of the first skiffs of snow. Each piece is patterned with waves as if the wood were fluid - tree growth seasoned by water.

DECEMBER 1974. JOURNAL ENTRY

Today it's raining, and the valley is socked in with fog, a fine sifting rain that you can barely see. The saskatoon bush is strung with crystal raindrops, like Christmas lights. The rock is the colour of slate, the plump moss a deep green, and the bark on pines has deepened to maroon. There are no mountains

Okanagan Lake is an existential exercise.

❦

As Scotty's crew nails the plywood sheathing around the perimeter walls, the basement, literally the 'sous-sol,' emerges-a big plywood box that looks like a Buddha, flat-lidded, low and squat. This could be one of those depression-era prairie houses, where people hunkered down in the basement for winter or years – until better times.

Scotty is not exactly Santa Claus - he's impatient, moves too fast, and swears a blue streak. But he's heaven-sent. As Christmas draws near, we have a basement, with a gun slot for a door.

Fresh snowfall, from the house site.

❦ 7 ❦

Framing Place

MARCH 13, 1916

On the 10th of February, the cold snap showed some signs of breaking ... But the frost had continued long enough to freeze the Lake from end to end — two feet in thickness at Penticton, 14 inches at Summerland. The thaw made little impression on the ice for some time, and there is still some loose ice drifting about the lake. Penticton has been cut off from the steamer service for about two months ...

– JOHN SUGARS, AN OKANAGAN HISTORY: THE DIARIES OF
ROGER JOHN SUGARS 1905-1916

We're above grade! (Is this a pass/fail system?) At the new year, we've made it up to ground level! Today the subfloor looks like a wooden lake. Damp from snowfall, its ripples and swirls of tree growth press like contoured topographies into 4-by-8 foot plywood sheets. Around the perimeter, booms of coded logs are stacked in place like a paint-by-number kit. You could string a rope around the edge of the corner vertical posts like a corral. Or a wrestling ring.

In another week, the first two walls look like the set of a Hollywood Wild West town, propped up in place. With all the walls up, the structure looks as if some invisible blade has scythed it horizontally in one fell swoop. Looking out from inside, each window frame has a different outlook - a ponderosa pine, the lake, the Kettle Valley Railway, Peachland – like an inverted Hiroshige, thirty-six views from Mount Fuji.

For the next two weeks, we haul the roof trusses out to the house site, our bodies hidden behind the strapping. If you were to look over from across the creek, all you'd see would be legs struggling downhill beneath 10-meter frames, like wonky fingers scissoring the path. These trusses frame the attic and provide a base for the cedar shingles. The backbone of the roof, they will extend and define the house, linking it to the sky. The roof will be the icing on the cake.

❦

"You, there! Reach over and nail this two-by-four. It's all right. I've got the ladder." Scotty barks as if it's a done deal.

Little John is pale, frozen at the top of the stepladder. He's up at the next-to-the-last step, which means that his shins barely connect with the top of the ladder. He's tottering back and forth, as if he's riding the Eiffel Tower, his eyes wide open, his mouth working. The man is scared shitless. In a slow calisthenics, his arms reach out to the side, then swing overhead.

"Keep 'er comin'," he gasps. His plaid shirt bellies out over his ample girth; his toque is pulled down against the cold of the winter morning. It's a good eight feet down to the plywood subfloor. His arms reach again towards the peak of the truss as if for divine countenance, and, sure enough, there's contact!

Rob angles the two-by-four out from the end wall, but Little John can't reach up to hammer the nail. There's nowhere to get a purchase, nothing to brace against to support his 250 pounds. The only exercise he's had for the past two months is bench-pressing beers at the pub.

The only thing steady is Scotty's voice. "Oh, Jesus! Do I have to come up there and do it myself?"

Little John flails out with the hammer. Connects. Gets the swing. Connects: one, two, three times. The truss is vertical, held in place by this 20-foot run of two-by-four. John slowly drops his hands, then climbs slowly down the steps of the ladder, sneaking looks at the truss, which looks like it is suspended from the sky.

We stare up at the truss, a giant reinforced frame extending from the front to the back wall. Two sides of an isosceles triangle edge up to meet in the middle of the sky. It is an act of God.

Perched on top of the walls, Jay and Rob tip the next truss skywards towards the end of the house and start walking it down the wall.

"So, where's the brace? I'll need some two-by-fours at this end," Scotty yells. I run outside, grab a long two-by-four and pivot back up the plank through the doorframe, like a tightrope walker with a balance bar.

Now Scotty's up the ladder. "All right, let's have it here." I lurch through the house towards him, like a jousting knight with a too-heavy sword. Scotty reaches down and grabs it.

"For the love of God, let's get moving," he snaps. "Do you want to get this done today, or sometime next year?"

The guy is sixty; we're thirty. We can't keep up.

By the end of the day all the trusses are strapped, stabilizing the logs stacked below, providing integrity and strength to the structure. Above our heads, a crosshatch of lumber subdivides the sky into two-foot-center lots.

🐿

We've set up an account with Beaver Lumber. It's like going to the old company store. They have everything you need. You don't have to pay directly for your purchases; you set up an account and 'sign' for them. It makes us feel like we're in business, that building a house is a proper job, as if we're contractors.

Hardware, clothing, gadgets, plumbing and electrical, flooring, lumber, automotive, office equipment, cleaning products, painting paraphernalia, plants and outdoor materials. When we go to Safeway for food, we're done in half an hour. But the hardware store? We're there half the day. We need joist hangers.

Hardware is guy candy.

❦

I study up.

At Beaver Lumber, products are functional and task-specific – the basis of skilled labour. Men shop here; it reinforces their masculinity. When I took home economics in high school, we learned how to cook stewed prunes and cream of tomato soup. Yech! Guys took 'shop'; girls learned how to shop. At Beaver Lumber, I can't identify three-quarters of the supplies on the shelves. The gear is labeled, but I don't know the pros and cons of different materials or brands.

Hardware exudes machismo. Men use tools and strength and know-how to get things done. They stand in the aisles, fingering the goods, rolling a tiny screw back and forth between thumb and forefinger in a dream state, visualizing the work they're going to do, and imagining which small jolt of metal will best serve the purpose.

Fastening one thing to another is an act of aggression. A nail punctures the wood in a single, direct hit, while a screw is threaded into its object, thereby gaining a stronger hold. He nails her, she is so screwed! It's all about sex and power.

Hmm. So the house is both erection and the object of sexual aggression? I reel at the sexuality of construction – couplings, male and female connections, the driving of steel into wood. And hardware! The house is a product of piercings and penetrations, all in the name of craft, of making a home.

🦌

The perky days of February and March coincide with shingling the roof, which consists of nailing cedar shingles along the one-by-four strapping that now spans the trusses. The idea of an aluminum roof has lost out to the aesthetics of cedar. At the end of winter, the wisps of bunchgrass and sponges of moss surrounding the house are an unlikely medium for fire. Granite doesn't burn.

Picture this! Fitted out in turtleneck, sweatshirt, plaid jacket, jeans, work boots, work gloves and a toque, legs hooked under the strapping, I'm perched high up on the trusses, trying not to look down six metres to the ground. The lake shimmers with the slight breeze; beneath me, the plywood floor of the house disappears row by row as we overlap shingle on shingle.

The shingles are rough and irregular, as if combed with steel wool teeth. The roof angles out over the edge, jutting over the rounded edges of the logs, a new infusion of rainforest cedar to this arid place. The deep fresh smell of cedar converges with the clean, fresh air of almost-spring. By summer, this wood will be dry and dusty, its coastal sap sucked dry.

🦌

West Kootenay Power and Light string lines for power and phone up to the house from the public road below. After months conjuring up alternative energy sources, from pinwheeled poles for wind power to waterwheeled turbines in the creek, Jay is resigned to the status quo.

We meet the West Kootenay guy down at the main road and plod uphill discussing the placement of power poles. He's gasping for breath by the time we reach the falls. Jay turns to him. "We want to put the cables underground the rest of the way," he explains. "So we won't have to see the wires from the house."

"The rest of the way...?" The guy is digesting this. He cranes to look up the steep pitch, then down at the waterfall sluicing through rocky bluffs. There is no road uphill, no house in sight.

As we stagger up the last steep pitch, we motion to the cleft in the rock wall, pointing to the golden cedar logs of the cabin. The guy slowly shakes his head. "All right. But how did you get this here?"

❧

In the spring, my sister Polly's friend Pete comes to build kitchen cabinets. He has an easy laugh and an even easier temper. Every morning it's the same routine: we wake up, scrabble breakfast together and fix lunch; Pete goes out a few minutes early to start his truck; a few moments of silence are shredded by a torrent of blasphemy.

"For the love of Jesus, what the hell is it today, you sonofabitching piece of shit! Should have junked you years ago, but I'm too damn sentimental. Now, let's just try it again."

Following moments of silence, there is a chorus: humm uh umm uh, rrgh, RRRGGGGHHH, umm uh ummmmmmmmhhhh! , which repeats twice, and then the door slams, and Pete's blue plaid shirt and gray chinos dangle over the engine's intestines.

It's not clear who is more temperamental, Pete or the truck. Sometimes there is the roar of engine, but sometimes there is only Pete, spewing words so loud, vitriolic and creative that people all the way across the lake in Summerland probably reel from the impact.

"Do you think we should say something to him?" I ask Jay. "We could get kicked out of town if this keeps up."

"It's entertainment. Everybody has times like this."

❧

Our neighbour Eleanor — spiritual, idealistic, and artistic — is a foil to my pragmatism. Her cedar-clad cottage has evolved in fits and starts, with direction from more than one contractor. Today, in the early spring sunshine, she sits outside her front porch, and plops a muddy handful of clay on the potting wheel. "My first priority is getting back to my work. Pottery sustains me." Then, as an afterthought, "I'm so fed up with building!"

"But Eleanor, we'll move in soon," I syrup along in a rare Pollyanna moment. " Then we'll be able to get back to our lives ..."

(What does that mean? Building the house has become my life.)

"You don't know how I've missed this," she sighs, and sits back on her stool. Poised over the potting wheel, she lifts her head impatiently, the sun glinting from her eyes, clay streaking her face and smock, her hands a dried putty of slurry. "Now if you'll excuse me..."

I step back as she kicks up the wheel.

❦

Pete's cabinets are just about done. He also builds us a big plywood 'armoire', a closet that looks a lot like a doublewide coffin.

Dropping in one day, Scotty ambles over to Jay. "Think you might need a wee hand with some of those other cabinets?"

❦

Scotty's back at our house with his carpenter, Andy. Now we have:

Cedar shelves in the dining room;

Bookshelves in our workrooms;

A railing at the stair opening; stairs to the basement;

Railings and a bench on the porches.

The last day he's in a hurry and cuts the risers for the front porch too short, so you stumble trying to go up or down the steps. He tries to fiddle the cut, but it's too late. He's gone.

❦

By spring, 1975, we're ready to move in, to "take possession" of a house that already possesses us. We cart the furniture out the path in tractor loads. The fir-dappled parking lot looks like a theatre set sprinkled with props – lamps, tables, bookshelves and chairs. Dan Harris and his brother Frank sling one end of the old kidney-shaped sofa into the tractor cart, where it hangs precariously during its ride out to the house. Robbie and Joanne carry kitchen chairs over their heads. Frank cantilevers the piano from the back of the tractor cart, cradling it as it swings down the trail. He and Dan hoist it up to the front porch, and we slide it into the living room.

By the end of the day, we are home!

Chute Creek Falls in winter.

PART TWO
Settlement

It needs a hardier stock of womankind - both physically and mentally... to stand the loneliness and hardships of this western life, but oh! How the country needs women strong in character, gentle in words and ways, to soften while they strengthen the rougher manners of the men.

— HOBNOBBING WITH A COUNTESS AND OTHER OKANAGAN ADVENTURES:
THE DIARIES OF ALICE BARRETT PARKE. EDITOR, JO FRASER JONES.

❦ 8 ❦
Systems: Kinetics and Hydraulics

As the steamer drew into the large government wharf... its passengers were met with a friendly welcome, for everyone turned out each night after supper to meet the boat and greet any newcomers... Although they were in a strange country... the new family felt at home almost right away.

You no sooner got your things into the house, than Mrs. Gillespie came to invite you to the Unity Club, which all the women in the town belonged to. Almost the first thing she would say was: 'What can you do? Can you sing, can you recite, can you do any solo dancing?

– BETTY CLOUGH, "REMINISCENCES OF NARAMATA," OKANAGAN HISTORY

Our friends Robbie and Joanne have been care-taking Paradise Ranch at the end of the road. Robbie shows up at our place one morning breathing hard, his jean jacket awry, glasses fogged, long hair busting loose from its ponytail. "You'll never guess where I've been."

We sit out on the porch, barely warmed by the morning light. The story spills out. "At 5:00 this morning the phone rings. It's Everett."

Robbie has been hanging out with the Harrises, moving irrigation pipes and helping with fencing.

Everett never calls us. I'm curious. "So what does he want at that hour?"

"Says there's a herd of elk just up above their place, and they're getting into the orchard. Making a mess of things. If we keep it quiet, we can probably knock one off, even though it's out of season. Wants to see if I can give him a hand."

Robbie's a vegetarian.

"So I throw on some clothes. It's still damned cold, but almost light. I jump in the truck and tear up to Harrises. He's got a whole posse there – the Harris kids of course, and Victor, even Mitch O'Neill. Everett goes tearing off in his truck, followed by Mitch and Victor; Danny jumps in with me."

Robbie starts to laugh, "Well, he led us on a merry goose chase. First we tear down to the ranch, 'cuz he says the elk were heading downhill. We're 'scoping the gullies, and down over the cliffs. Nothing at the lake, so we take off again and race up to Glenfir, to the train tracks. Drive up and down, in and out of the trucks, sneaking through the woods like Robin's Merry Men. Still no sign."

Jay sits quietly, nursing his tea. "Then what happened?"

"Well, we tear up and down the road, back towards town, stopping and starting. Everett's got his gun handy at the back of the truck. Still nothing. No sign. By now it's about 7:30. I need my coffee. We're all standing there with the trucks parked at the Chute Lake turnoff. I say to Everett: 'How many elk are in this herd?'

"He mutters: 'At least ten. Good sized.' He's acting weird, more so than normal, stomping around, kind of agitated.

"Dan says to him, 'Look, Dad, it's been an early start. Maybe we should let it go for the day. We'll keep a look out.'

"I chime in," says Rob. 'Yeah, it's still pretty early in the season. What is it, the first of April?' Then it hits us! Dan yelps, 'Dad, how could you do this?' Frank is so pissed off that he stomps to his truck and blasts off down the road. The rest of us stand there in disbelief.

"But Everett just starts giggling, that manic, crazy laugh. He jumps in his truck, tosses an 'April Fool!' out the window, and rips off down the road."

❧

Now that winter is over and we have a basement, it's time to store the snow tires. I roll one along the path from the parking lot towards the house, as it picks up steam. Soon I'm jogging to keep up with it. I'm running full out when the tire slips away from my hand and veers off and over the side of the path. SPROING! SPROING!

It bounces higher and higher down the steep hillside as I skid to a stop on the trail. The tire dribbles down the fall line, gallops past phone poles, glances off rocks and stumps and springs beneath towering pine trees. It disappears into steep rugged terrain, headed towards the creek. I scramble downhill after it, but there is no trace, just the riparian confusion of the creek in early runoff.

Next November, after the leaves have dropped, we find the tire, where it nestles among boulders in its new home in the creek bed.

❧

We begin staining wood walls and ceilings, and dry-walling the interior walls. Now that we're "home", we even start to take time off from working on the house. One evening in May we ask Scotty and his wife Noreen over for dinner while my dad is visiting. Scotty is polite but restrained. He and my dad don't have much in common.

After dinner, I play a recording of one of my father's favorite Scottish folk songs, Road to the Isles. "Da da dum, da da da da daadadaadah Daa Dah" fills the woodlot living room. Dad jumps up from the table and takes my hand. Point, point, then walk, walk, walk (pause) then point and point, and then we turn. We know this dance by heart. We glide through the living room, and turn, and back again, in time to the music.

Out the window, Loch Lomond stretches to the south, fringed in sage and bunchgrass. "Well, I never ..." sputters Scotty. "For the love of God, who would ever think we'd be listening to Road to the Isles in this place!"

He turns to my father. "How did you learn this?" Dad laughs while Scotty shakes his head. "I don't know the bloody steps and I grew up with the music!"

❦

In early June, the night is still pitch black when the alarm goes off. It's 3:30 a.m. We fumble to get dressed. Ten minutes later we're standing by the side of the truck, listening. To something, but what?

"Half a minute. That's it!" Jay says, jumping back in the truck. He's pretty excited. "Here, you hold the report sheet. This is Stop One. Nothing to report."

We tear off down the road for exactly half a mile. He pulls over to the side and jumps out. This time there's a little more action. "Song sparrow, robin." Then quiet. "Half a minute. All right, we're off." He's taking this seriously.

The next stop, we both hear the twittering of a pygmy nuthatch. "Tee dee, ee-dee, tee-dee, wee-bee, wee-bee." Maybe things will improve with the light.

This year we're involved in the British Columbia Nest Record scheme, recording the number and species of nesting birds in a given area. Our route is from the back of Summerland, working westward past Osprey Lake to Princeton.

Next stop, another half a mile. Another half a minute. "Shhh," Jay whispers. "O.K. I've got it. That's a Townsend's Solitaire like the one nesting near the house."

At Osprey Lake, a truck tears past, headlights glaring, scuttling the pebbles and dust at the edge of the road. The guy leans on the horn. He doesn't care if it's a fox or a song sparrow. He's probably on his way to a dawn construction start.

By 9:15, we have:

Red-tailed Hawk	California Quail
American Coot	Clark's Nutcracker
Osprey	Green-winged Teal
Killdeer	White-crowned Sparrow
Song Sparrow	Lewis's Woodpecker
Northern Flicker	Red-winged Blackbird
Townsend's Solitaire	Western Kingbird
Barn Swallow	Violet-green Swallow
Mallard	Common Raven
American Crow	Western Bluebird
Mountain Chickadee	Black Capped Chickadee
Pygmy Nuthatch	Red-breasted Nuthatch
Rufous-sided Towhee	American Goldfinch
Black-billed Magpie	Audubon's Warbler
Brewer's Blackbird	Say's Phoebe
Canada Goose	Bufflehead
Turkey Vulture	American Kestrel
American Robin	Brewer's Blackbird

Breakfast in Princeton.

Life at the Granite Farm is rooted in biophysics. Even though we've been here for over a year, some things are still new. Like sagebrush mariposa lily, Calochortus macrocarpus.

This species was once widespread ... Native people and early settlers harvested the thick,
fleshy bulbs in early spring and ate them raw, steamed, boiled or pit-cooked. They were
dug before the plants flowered in late spring and early summer... The genus derives its
name from the Greek kalo, 'beautiful,' and chortos, 'grass,' referring to the lovely flowers...
'Mariposa' is Spanish for butterfly—the wide, spreading petals resemble broad-winged
butterflies.

— PARISH, COUPÉ AND LLOYD. PLANTS OF SOUTHERN INTERIOR
BRITISH COLUMBIA

Let's say you are walking uphill, through grasslands tufted in rabbitbrush
and sage. You're still watching out for ticks, but the season's past; the day
is lush with birdsong and bee buzz and the spatter of creek. A soft mauve
tulip-like bloom lolls atop a long slender stem, three petals cupping the
center like cats' ears. Say you stop, glance around, and suddenly notice
that the field is pinked, purpled, with soft, satin flowers. You don't pick
them, because they don't last, and you want them to seed so that next
year this field will bloom with rosy, violet, powder pink goblets of
mariposa lily, and you will be born again.

Life settles into the everyday as we wrangle domestic life into a wilder
place. At summer solstice, Jay's parents come to visit. It's a long trip for
all of us and almost dark by the time we drive up the hill. Jay's dad, who
loathes walking anywhere, teeters out the path to our wilderness hotel.
We walk in the front door, turn on the oven, and throw in trays of
barbecued chicken to heat. Everyone has another drink.

    EEPP! All of a sudden tiny squeaks peep from the oven, as if the
breeding birds have come home to roost. (To roast?) I open the broiler

tray to find a mother mouse scurrying to extract her babies from the sudden heat. Dinner goes downhill from there.

❧

JULY 15, 1911. FINTRY, B.C.

The Saskatoon bush (Amelanchier Alnifolia) grows chiefly on dry, sunny hillsides or flats... In the early spring it has a beautiful white blossom on every branch...The fruit is... a purple-red black berry about as large as a big black currant & grows in pendulous clusters. It is very good flavoured & juicy, is very nice eaten either raw, or cooked.

– JOHN SUGARS. AN OKANAGAN HISTORY: THE DIARIES OF
ROGER JOHN SUGARS 1905-1919

JULY, 1975. NARAMATA, B.C.

Saskatoon is the fruit of pioneers. It offers shade, beauty, and white fluffy hillsides in April and May. Berries are food for humans, bears, and birds, the source of luscious royal purple dye. In bloom, saskatoon is a bridal bower – white, frothy, and fresh. All around the house, saskatoon roots drill through rock cleavage, seeking moisture that dissipates under the heat lamp of summer. By August, dry toothy leaves sprinkle the hard baked earth.

What happens to June brides in this hot place? How long until they wither?

❧

The days melt away in a stream of house/work and episodic events. Mid-summer, there is a knock at the front door. Two men in suits, with sweaty pink faces, stand on the porch, small briefcases in hand. "Good morning, Ma'am. We were in the neighbourhood, and thought we would stop by."

Oh no. It couldn't be. The younger man is pulling a small newspaper from his briefcase. Yikes! It is!! Watchtower. "We thought you might be interested in some of our literature," says the older of the two, turning from me to scan the porch and the blue of the lake. "Perhaps living here, you may wish to contemplate some of the bigger questions."

"Well, indeed, yes, I do, but I'm really not interested in this material." I should ask them in for tea, at least offer them something to drink. But they're already turning away from the front door. "How did you find your way to this house?" I ask.

"Your kind neighbor, Mr. Harris, suggested you might be interested in our materials," says the younger man, walking stiffly down the stairs.

❦

Later that summer, we're at Violet Gibbard's on Arawana Road. Violet, an old timer in Naramata, maintains the records for the British Columbia Nest Record Scheme. As we walk around, entranced by her extensive garden, Jay muses aloud, "We're thinking of putting up signs to protect the wildlife. Yesterday a couple of guys rode dirt bikes through our place, all the way up from the public road at the bottom. They said they didn't know it was private property."

Violet nods.

Jay continues, " But we don't know kind of signs to put up. We don't want to offend people, or get the signs shot down right away. If people have always been able to walk around this place, we don't want to suddenly restrict them."

Violet lifts her eyebrows. She doesn't understand.

He stops, considers this, and continues: "In fact, if they don't disturb the wildlife, it's all right with us for other people to walk around. What about "Treat this land with respect"?" he asks Violet.

"Absolutely not," Violet replies. She nods her head with certainty. "No Trespassing! No Hunting! That's how you protect the place!

⚜

Our neighbour Eleanor has moved into her house across the creek. In addition to her prolific artistic skills, Eleanor is a diviner! A water witch!

One day in August we're walking down the road when Eleanor stoops to pick up a long stick lying under the cottonwoods, and hands it to me. "Take it in your hands where it branches, and hold it horizontally in front of you," she urges.

Nothing happens. "See. I just don't have the touch." I hand the stick back to Eleanor and she walks back uphill, retracing my steps.

Just past the little run-off to the creek, where the road winds beneath a thicket of alder, she stops, her arms stretched down. "There!" she exclaims.

Eleanor is wearing her straw hat with the ribbon. Her artist's smock wafts in the morning breeze as she clutches the stick, which is pulled down as if it wants the earth, almost wrenching itself from her hands.

"Put your hands here, next to mine," she urges.

I reach over to place my hands on hers and feel a current, a charge greater than gravity. Am I imagining this?

Eleanor shrugs her shoulders. "Sometimes you have to just let it come to you." Then she turns towards her house.

⚜

By August, Chute Creek is barely a dribble. The creek is the only year-round stream at our end of the road, and, except for the lake, the major source of irrigation. In an agricultural community dependent on water for orchards, grapes and other crops, its supply is critical. According to local accounts, the dam at the lake was controlled by shotgun during the war. Today there is little formal regulation of water along this irrigation system.

The cistern will be located on a rock ledge, tucked up and behind the house, and capable of gravity feed. It will be rectangular in shape, 10- by 12- by 9-feet, capable of holding over a thousand cubic feet of water. That should take us through dry spells in the summer or the winter, when the creek ices up.

One day in early September, the first of three concrete trucks throbs up the logging road, its huge churning tank drowning the trickle of the creek. George, the driver, throttles it into place just above our parking space. He runs the hoses across the hillside and over to the forms, pieces of gray plywood woven with rebar and twist-tied together into a massive open box.

The pipes twitch and bulge as the sludge flows over to the forms.

Blaagh! Caplooogh! Schlump! After half an hour, the snorting pump begins to jerk back and forth erratically in Jay's hands, writhing like a huge snake as it disgorges thicker, chunkier blobs of concrete. As the mix erupts from the pipe, Jay tries to slump it towards Rob on the other side of the cistern. "Pull it over! We want to get an even coating."

Hanging over the side of the form, Robbie struggles to pull a hoe-load towards him, but it's too heavy. The concrete belches out the pipe, too lumpy and stiff to blend with the looser slurry in the forms. Jay can barely hold on as the pipe jerks explosively, back and forth, up and down like a bucking bronco.

We scream at George, who's back around the hillside with the concrete truck. He tears out the path, shouting, "Christ, I don't know what's wrong. We'll have to unhook her."

Darting back and forth atop the forms, Jay yells, "But we've just started! There's only about three inches of concrete in there. Why can't you just loosen the load?"

George barks back: "It's setting up on me! These trucks are only good for a couple of hours. I'm gonna' have to dump her!"

We drop our tools and scramble down the hill, out to the road where the groaning, belly-rolling truck has become now a rotisserie of concrete sludge. George slumps to the ground, beating his fists on the rocky ground.

He sobs, "The mix is too thick. I've got to call the company. The other trucks will already be on the road!" He crawls back to his feet and scrambles downhill to phone from the house.

At the truck, the pipe continues to flail and writhe while the load cycles around and around, groaning and screeching like a wounded animal. Joanne yells above the din, "Why can't we turn the thing off?"

"It's got to keep rolling, or it'll thicken up," mumbles Jay. He throws his shovel to the ground. "We're doomed! All that stuff in the forms is setting up."

He turns and trudges slowly back uphill towards the cistern. Over his shoulder, he shouts: "We'll never get the rest poured by hand. Even if we do, it'll never bond!"

On the hillside, chunks of concrete are spewed everywhere – stochastic flows, rough slabs, boulders, and tubes like elephant poop, pattycakes. Rock on rock.

George packs up the pumper and grinds downhill.

Proud Mary keeps on rolling!

A plastic swimming pool becomes our temporary cistern for storing water. Pink dolphins frolic on bright blue plastic under a patch of scabby pine. After we build a path to the cistern site, we cart tractor loads of sand, gravel and cement up from the parking lot. Long outdoor extension cords bring power up from the house.

We rent an electric mixer, and shovel-by-shovel, load-by-load, scramble up the hill, around rocks, and up and down ladders. Friends come to help again: Eleanor and Meryl, Stewart and Leslie, Robbie and Joanne. Concrete splashes down into the forms. Shplat!! Around the perimeter, we mix it back and forth, smoothing it into one big box of concrete – seams, cracks and all.

In two weeks, the forms are filled. A week later, we remove them. The cistern's geology unfolds: ragged pebbled stripes layer in a helter-skelter sedimentation of pours. Conglomerates of slurry bunch with chunks of porous concrete at the bottom; seams of aggregate run at diagonals where they weren't mixed in; pockmarks of air holes crater the surface.

We parge the inside of the cistern, and Jay frames a roof with a trap door, then tarpapers and shingles it. He marks red paint lines on the inside wall indicating 500- and 1000-gallon gradients, laddering up to 7500 gallons. Outside, Our Lady of Chute Creek is enshrined in thin, plywood sheets.

The pumper sues the cement company. The cement company sues the concrete pumper. Nobody comes out ahead.

This bright autumn day, Eleanor has organized an Okanagan Mountain hike. As the group slogs up the path from Commando Bay, our leader Victor Wilson charges ahead, pounding a stiff pace up the hard packed trail with his walking staff, old army knapsack pulled snugly against his back. His white hair is trimmed short, and his posture is erect – shoulders back, chest strong, shirt tucked snugly into his khaki pants. He is the very model of a modern major general. He pulls a handkerchief from his pocket and wipes his brow, waiting for the rest of us to straggle uphill. 'The Colonel' speaks with precision: "At the head of this canyon, where we meet the Wild Horse Canyon trail, we'll stop for a break."

Today happens to be Yom Kippur, the Jewish Day of Atonement. I suspect that this hike may qualify. My grandmother immigrated to New

York from Eastern Europe in 1911, from poverty and pogroms. When I was a child, she dispensed soft orange marshmallow treats to New World grandchildren in her dark, stuffy Bronx apartment. She never talked about her past, her husband's death or her penniless early years in a new country, speaking no English, with two babies to support.

A quarter-century later, on the far side of the continent, my new neighbours never complain. They munch rosy-cheeked apples, whinny at one another's wit, and press on up the path. I drag myself up the dusty trail propelled by the chirp of British accents, and think about what it means to come to a new country.

❦

It's hot on the Wild Horse Canyon trail. The leaves are brittle and parched and the dust from our boots silts the air. Heat blasts from canyon walls back into our faces, stifles conversation, and raises clouds of dust as we shuffle along. As we crest to the southern swing of the lake in the late afternoon, Victor pulls out his canteen and takes a long swig, then, far ahead of the rest of the group, pauses to talk to Jay and me. His glacial eyes are calm and cool.

"I did have something I wanted to tell you two. I thought you should know that I've purchased the property adjacent to yours." He turns away to continue briskly uphill.

"What?" I say, speeding to catch up with him. "You mean the Northwood land? We didn't know that it was for sale..."

Jay is right behind me, breathing hard. "But that's huge, hundreds of acres. We hoped that piece would become a part of the Park someday."

Victor fixes us with those icicle-blue eyes. "Better the devil you know than the devil you don't know."

🐾 9 🐾
Wintering Over

The pride of every woman was her cook stove. The shiny steel surface, and the polished nickel-plated trim depicted the care it was given...It was commonplace to see a large kettle of water steaming merrily away on the stove... I well remember how good it felt to come downstairs on a cold winter morning and sit on the oven door to warm my back.

— ALICE E. EMENY. "THE KITCHEN RANGE," OKANAGAN HISTORY

The October sun advertises the day and defines the landscape. As I drive into town, lemon leaves of wild rose and willows flutter in every draw and ditch. Elderberries above the cattle guard dangle mauve fruit pale as poison and thick as caviar. Mellow yellow cottonwoods flap along Naramata Creek. Up and down the lake it's a fall fair, a cheap thrills carnival of color.

By 4:00 the sun has already dropped beneath a ridge of clouds above Brent Mountain. Its descent backlights the clouds, swathing the hills in golden light.

🐾

By early November, for our first winter in the house, we have electricity, water from the cistern, and wood-fired heat! Three wood-burning stoves

— a King heater, a Franklin fireplace and a cook stove — supplement the electric baseboards. Their stainless steel pipes poke through the shingle roof like sputnik vents.

HEATING INVENTORY

STOVE #1. The Franklin fireplace isn't easy to install.

"O.K., now, let's slide it over here. We need to attach the vent." Jay coaxes the stove into position.

He stops abruptly, his hands pointing to the ceiling. "I don't believe it! The truss runs right over the stove."

Jay is heated up. "I can't believe I didn't catch that."

Now he's smoking! "We'll have to put an "L" in the pipe."

He's on fire. "There goes the draft!"

He's right. Every night, clouds of smoke sneak, puff and billow erratically from the Franklin. The fireplace smokes when we light it, when we close the grill, when logs roll out of place, of even if it's just having a bad night. Daily particulate consumption skyrockets. There's a new "tickle" in my throat.

STOVE #2. Betsy is an off-white Monarch cook stove from the 1920's, with corroded nickel-trim and a rusted iron cook plate. She looked forlorn in the farmer's yard in Keremeos when we rescued her, a far cry from her glory days.

What was it like to can fruit in July on a wood stove?

"I'm never going to cook on this thing," I state emphatically. Nostalgia only goes so far.

Jay nods grudgingly. The crimped vertebrae of Betsy's rusty pipe crowns the stove, disconnected to the shiny stainless steel circle of pipe protruding through the ceiling, as if there's been a 'stop work' order on the project.

There has.

STOVE #3. The King heater in the front hallway is the main source of heat. Procedure: scrunch up balls of newspaper, add pieces of old pine bark and kindling from under the porch, wedge in pine and fir logs. Light the paper. Shut the door tight.

WHOOSH! Clank, clank, clank, CLANK, CLANK!

As the heater gets up to speed, the box and frame adjust.

When the stove bites into new wood, it comes into its own, creaking and groaning, settling into a good wave of heat that wafts like a mirage from the top of the grill. Sometimes there is a sudden snort of back draft, a massive exhalation signifying insufficient air. Other times, the pinholes at the "U" in the stack glare red, which could indicate a chimney fire. How can a mere caution of metal pipe insulate such a roaring inferno?

I put my hands above the grill to feel the warmth. The stack funneling up through the ceiling is wicked hot. I look at the ceiling. A foot below the tongue-and-groove cedar ceiling, the pipe is double insulated. But I'm surrounded by wood – furniture, cedar bookcases and cabinets, cedar walls and ceiling, a fir floor, fir trusses and cedar shingles.

I know that heating with wood is local, cheap and efficient. But I'm never easy with the non-fiction of wood heat. I'm more comfortable with fiction, with baseboard heaters that mean a river has been dammed somewhere else to trickle into heat at my feet.

As winter sets in, I'm still absorbing the lay of the land. The Granite Farm is sandwiched by the large expanse of Paradise Ranch to the north, and Chute Creek to the south. The house is tucked among rocks, hundreds of feet above the main road; coming home is an exercise of habit as well as faith.

You drive up the logging road, park the car and walk down the path. As you round the hillside, a gabled kitchen porch and cedar logs materialize on a rocky plateau. Rabbitbrush and sage and saskatoon rim the front 'yard'; in back, rocky hills clamber up, and up again. When you're indoors, the windows take you back outside, into ragged cliffs and scattered bunchgrass and pines that are reason enough to call this home.

The house may fit the place, but becoming part of the 'community' is more difficult. Without children or an agricultural connection, it is difficult to find a niche. Our friends are other newcomers. We visit Alex and Jeannie at least once a week, and check in on Eleanor as we drive up the hill. Robbie and Joanne are close by, and other friends from Vancouver have moved to Summerland.

Now that we're living in the house, people rarely stop by to visit. I admit, we are off the beaten path. And the house is no longer a work-in-progress. Moving into the new house has made it private. It's time to start looking for work. Jay is writing freelance, but I have yet to bridge my way back to the workforce. I've joined the Naramata Choir and Jay is active with the South Okanagan Naturalist's Club. We hike with the Penticton Outdoors Club. Why do I feel so lonely?

❦

NARAMATA CENTRE
OCTOBER 26, 1975

Mrs. Melody Lewis
R. R. #1
Naramata, B. C. V0H 1N0

Dear Melody:

Thank you very much for your letter of the 15th of October with the proposal for a dance program here at the Centre. I read your letter to our recent Program Committee meeting and it was very well received indeed. We are impressed with your extensive experience in contemporary and folk dance, your teaching experience, as well as your academic work with dance criticism.

We are presently in the process of putting together our schedule for next summer, spring, and fall, and we will be in touch with you in the fairly near future to see how we can fit your ideas into our forthcoming programs.

In any event I wanted to write and tell you that we very much like your proposal and sincerely hope to be able to work with you.

Yours sincerely,

Peter Houston
Staff Associate

❦

JOURNAL ENTRY. NOVEMBER, 1975

A huge cloudy overcast blankets the sky to the south in a sober gray that I am learning to associate with Okanagan winters. A temperature inversion socks in daily over the valley due to carbon dioxide from cars, wood stoves, and the burning of orchard prunings. The sunshine winter days recorded by early settlers have been muffled by a seasonal lint-gray cold.

Temperatures are dropping fast. Even before the bears have denned, I am hibernating: progressing from one cup of cocoa to the next as I putter around the house, putting on fat. This morning the world beyond the cliff drizzles into fog: diffuse, featureless and infinite. There is no lake. A bedraggled kestrel perches on the snag in front of the house.

By afternoon, when I finally get outside, the day is almost done. A ping-pong moon bounces into the sky up over the railroad tracks. Coyotes begin to yelp in a tight, tiny, wavering siren. I squeal back, "Yip, yip, yiiiiiippp!" Then comes the reply - sharp, squeaky cries, shrill and sharp, perhaps young coyotes. The nightly cloak of darkness floods the hillside.

🦌

We've tried to minimize our impact on the environment with a non-obtrusive building and the conservation of natural habitat. We plant drought tolerant shrubs so we won't use much water or alter the terrain. Nonetheless, we've encroached on territory occupied by others.

Rumors of resistance surface in an alternative conservation initiative:

October 22, 1975   Full Moon Rising
Minutes of the Predator Control Board
North Naramata, B.C.
Present: Coyote, Black Bear, Cougar, Rattlesnake,
Great Horned Owl, Golden Eagle
Regrets: Bobcat, Bald Eagle, Ferret

The meeting was convened and chaired by Coyote. Owl served as recorder. Minutes from the last meeting and the night's agenda were approved.

The meeting opened with a general discussion concerning increasing predation on indigenous species by homo sapiens. PCB members report the escalation of hostile activities, including habitat destruction, illegal hunting, trapping and poaching, harassment and physical assault, fencing and restriction of traditional foraging corridors. As noted in greater detail below, all pose an increased risk to predator survival.

1. Coyote reports increased incidents of assault, ranging from shooting and poison to more barbaric forms of attack. Coyote is especially concerned about the 'war on the wild', especially the gratuitous violence associated with increased access to firearms and poison;

2. Cougar and bobcat express concern for increases in hound-assisted tracking hunts. They argue that these involve the recruitment of domestic species to human objectives, the subversion of strategic bonds between feline and canine species and the reduction of habitat;

3. Black bear documents significant increases in predator activity against juveniles and young, especially when food supplies are scarce during pre- and post-denning activity;

4. Several members (bobcat, cougar, bear) report expanded human encroachment during all seasons. Human 'free range' increases road access, ATV and snowmobile activity, diminishing animal safety. The extension of hunting seasons is also unsupported by PCB data.

The motion brought before the PCB at the preceding meeting is formally approved and carried. The motion as approved reads: "The range and technical capabilities of human predators in traditional non-human habitat should be restricted." With a count of paws and claws, the motion was adopted unanimously and is now the basis for future Predator Control Policy.

Discussion of potential mitigation measures for predator management include the introduction of "culls," approval of traditional subsistence predation rights, restrictions on human encroachment into traditional wildlife areas, standards for so-called 'protected areas', and the formation of a new wildlife authority 'with teeth'.

The next meeting will be held first at the full moon, next spring, following hibernation. Venue: TBA.

🐾

Choir practice highlights my week. Every Tuesday at 7:30, some fifty people of every age and voice drift into the Naramata Centre. My first public performance is the Christmas concert.

"You can probably fit Susan Wollstrom's gown, Melody. Why don't you take this home with you and let me know how it works," smiles Roberta Bingham, passing me a long, elegant cream coloured gown done up in plastic.

Wow! I carry it out to the house, careful not to let it drag on the path. This is the most elegant dress I've ever worn, with a fitted waist and a full skirt that swoops to the floor. It's the prom dress, the wedding dress, the dress-up dress I always eschewed. I waltz back and forth in front of the mirror. I shoulder into the forest-green top-coat. Elegant!

Even if it is a bit Anne Murray.

What happened to Susan Wollstrom? Why did she quit the choir?

❧

Carol McGibney is the director. She's Irish. And animated, funny, sharp, vivacious and warm. Her short curly brown hair pixies bright brown eyes and rosy cheeks. "Tonight we're going to warm up with John Denver," she says, waving the music for Angela's Waltz in front of us.

Like my woodstove, the choir cranks up.

"We dance through a faahhhhrrrrr–essssssssttt."

Carol is waving at the tenors. "Let's pep it up a bit, move it along." Her head is nodding, arms forging a quicker beat, hands beckoning. "Up, up, pick it up!" She beckons to Laura, the accompanist, to pick up the pace, stirring the air with her baton as if she's whipping cream,

I steal a look over at the tenors. No wonder they're slow. Some of them are older than my dad! Can they even read the words? Few of us can read music. Most of the time we're reading Carol. Her voice and gestures pull us together, forging one song from all-over-the-map voices.

"No, no, no. Stop right there!" Carol's face heats up to cherries. She motions to Laura to stop, and then steams at the choir.

"What do you think you're singing? Have any of you looked at this music?"

She is looking right over my head at the basses. "What happened at section practice?" Her face has definitely moved to plum. "This was supposed to be an easy warm-up. I hate to think about the Christmas music. We have a concert soon, and this sounds like pea soup!"

Carol nods to Laura, and we're off again. This time it flows. It simmers. It cooks! We sound like hot buttered rum, warm and toasty and syrupy.

"...through cedar and moonlight." Ahh, that's better. My thoughts drift. And sagebrush and pine trees. Our voices waltz through the forest, blend with coyotes, blanket the far west. The village voice!

🦌

By late November, the hillsides of Summerland are sprinkled with icing-sugar snow. The frozen bare ground of our path is etched in fronds of feathery frost. Ice forms around the sides of the falls, clamping the last trace routes of the creek into fixed points. The outer spray region is marbled with ice.

The bite of winter crunches the days, reducing the world to this small plateau. Nothing else exists but the house and a gray horizon. One day the snow swirls down in waves like shorebirds above the sea. By early afternoon it expands to large, wispy flakes, with intricate geometries like cut-outs from third grade.

But there is no schoolyard rush of toques and boots, no shrieks and snowballs and sopping wet gloves dripping in the cloakroom. This snow muffles sight and sound. By late afternoon, bb-shots of snow blast the rock and scour the screen of gray that has erased the lake. The wind hones the snow into crystals icy and sharp. Just before night falls, you can see the lake again and make out the mountains on the other side.

One afternoon, in a day that has always been dusk, with snow still filtering down, Jay and I ski down to Eleanor's. Our skis sink into bottomless soft white as we flounder in the direction of the path, plodding downhill to the creek. Under deep drifts, we can barely hear its gurgle.

In snow up to our thighs, we clamber along what once was the road, towards Eleanor's cabin. The tracks of our skis are a deep mauve, lit from within. Eleanor greets us at the door of Stonecrop, her little house, with freshly baked cookies. We sit together at the kitchen table, gazing out the window at the confetti of falling snow.

🦌

By December we need more firewood. Jay bends over the corpse of an old fir tree in his red wool jacket, toque, plastic goggles and earmuffs.

The racket of the chainsaw screeches into the afternoon, high-pitched and erratic, like an outboard engine or a ski machine, butchering the quiet of the day.

I am determined to learn how to use a chainsaw, but they are scary and dangerous. Up close, they screech like a dentist's drill. Chainsaws can stick in the wood, chuck splinters into your eyes, or kick loose and bronco back. A chainsaw is the definitive rural industrial instrument; it out- punks rock.

I stick with my autoharp.

♥

Tonight Joe Denton, who lives on the road to town, is throwing a winter solstice party. We usually meet Joe when he hitchhikes to town, grubby and bathed in an aura of garlic and sweat. Sometimes he drives a relic of a truck barely held together by baling wire. Joe has carved an orchard and garden from a bare hillside of Crown land; he works harder than just about anyone we know.

To get to Joe's you drive down the main road. Just past the old dump, where you hit pavement, you veer off into the bunchgrass and knapweed and sagebrush, following an old track that winds downhill.

Tonight a couple of old pickups browse atop the hill. A lighthouse moon beacons the field of illuminated snow. If it weren't for the snow and the full moon, it would be hard to even see Joe's place. But there it is: a tiny cabin overlooking the lake, windows glowing with candles and kerosene lamps. The beat of drums dimples the bitter night. The lake silvers out like an angel wing, reflecting the moonlight.

After slogging downhill through the snow, we stumble inside and take off our coats and boots. Sprawled on the floor around the fireplace are about twenty people, some of whom I know only by sight. There's Robin, the cute American, and Jean-Guy, the Quebecois guy who came out years ago to pick fruit and still lives in the cabin at the bend in the road, and Sonja, who lives with Joe, sweet and shy with big blue eyes. She smiles and beckons us across the room. We sit on the floor and drink beer and smoke enough dope to belong to the night and the scene. Guitars and drums and song weave everyone together in the rhythm and the place.

Joe's cabin is a tiny pod of kindred souls hanging on to one another in a place where, for the most part, nobody can afford to stay. People in this room know how to graft fruit trees, how to treat peach curl, how to fix irrigation pipes and where to pick mushrooms. Nobody belongs to the Fruit Grower's Co-op and most don't pay much, if anything, in taxes, but we all live here. The windows perspire with condensation, the floor throbs with drumbeats, and we are one breath.

Looking out the kitchen window on this cold winter morning, I can just make out the Little Tunnel on the Kettle Valley Railway. In 1915, the KVR began to carry freight and passengers from Vancouver to Nelson, but less than a century, the tracks are gone. The last passenger train ran in 1964, and freight trains were suspended in 1973. Our first winter in the house, Jay and I teach cross-country skiing, holding the class on the KVR tracks at Glenfir.

"Your glide can carry you forever." Jay tells his group. "With good pole action, and crisp snow conditions, you can really coast."

He pushes off on one leg, soaring along the track like the Skater's Waltz. "Now, leave your poles here, at one end," he urges, sticking his poles upright in the snow.

"Just push off on your skis, like you're skating!"

We all ski out towards the tunnel, about five kilometres each way. By the end of the class, Sven and Inge and their students are sweaty, tired and happy. They double-pole back to the house for treats.

♚

Cabin fever.

Leonard Cohen said, "it begins with your body, and soon it comes down to your soul." He was 'bushed' in downtown Montreal!

I don't want to go out. I don't want to go anywhere.

Jay is not bushed. "We're running out of firewood," he says, lacing his boots. "Guess I'd better buck up the old pine tree out back. I'll go get the chainsaw."

He buttons his jacket, avoiding my eyes, and grabs his work gloves. I'm too cold. "I'll be right out. I just want to finish this letter."

Three hours later, Jay is back at the front door, shaking the snow off his jacket, stomping his boots on the porch to dislodge the caked up snow, his arms full of firewood. He doesn't say anything.

I don't say anything.

♚

Imagine the gossip a century ago:

"Why is she moping around when there is so much to do? Her 'garden' this past summer was the laughing stock of the town. She planted nothing but flowers! She appears disinterested in the maintenance of her home, and wiles away the time peering at birds, or plinking at the piano. She not only lacks basic skills; she lacks pluck.

And why has she no children? One's offspring can be a productive addition to the household, and good company as well. Nor has she chickens, goats, or cows, all of which would surely contribute to the viability of her homestead. Her husband seems a nice man. Independent, like they all are, and capable of strong work. But he has chosen the wrong wife! This one has not the stomach for this life. Pity!"

♚

Jay sets up a cross-country ski track at the Chute Lake turnoff from the main road. He takes off in the morning with his skis, blue flagging tape and a pair of clippers and doesn't come back for hours. I think that the road is too low and the snow too shallow to set a track. You have to go up to Chute Lake to find all-winter snow. He's so stubborn!

❦

Jay's Side of the Story

I don't know what to think. Ever since we moved into the house, she's been moping. Just when we're ready to get some new projects going and make some new friends, she's thrown in the towel. There are so many things to do: stain the walls, finish the drywalling, paint the kitchen cabinets, finish the basement...

She doesn't even see how beautiful it is. I've set up a new cross-country course on crown land, but she won't even come to check it out. She complains that there's nothing to do, and that she doesn't have any friends.

❦

Things begin to look up:

NARAMATA CENTRE
JANUARY 28, 1976

Dear Melody:

We are pleased to inform you that we have been able to make space for your contemporary dance class during the summer session. Your class will be scheduled from 4 - 5:30 for the period from July 17-21. It will be open to all Naramata Centre participants, and we will also provide opportunities for local residents to take part as well.

We will be pleased to pay you an honorarium of $150 for this period, and look forward to having you among our Creative Arts staff. Let us know if there is any additional information we can provide to enhance your affiliation with the Centre. We look forward to having you among our staff.

Sincerely,

Peter Houston
Staff Associate

❧

Tonight, Carol stands in front of the altos, my section, at choir practice. "Let's take it one more time, from the bottom of page two," urges Carol, nodding us along.

We're singing, "Memories." Middle-aged people surround me, crooning about their youth. I feel like Barbra Streisand in the movie, The Way We Were, too abrupt and different to melt into this place.

"Is it just that everything seemed easy then?
Simple and so true, as if somehow ..."
How does this go?
(If I could only once more have that chance again?)
(If I could only get into your pants again?)
What are we singing about? Having an affair?
"But it's the mem'ries, we'll always dream of ....
Every time we dream of, the niiiiiight we met."
I'm practically in tears. Maybe singing with the choir is an exercise in nostalgia for a life I'll never have. As if you could pre-fabricate memory.

❧

This is the way we ~~used to be~~ are. Today the pipes are frozen so I have to haul water from the creek again. Jay is already working up at the cistern. I get dressed, grab two buckets, and force myself out the front door. The ground is frozen hard. It is colder than cold, so cold that I hold the air in my mouth before inhaling. My breath puffs like smoke as I climb up the path and down the road over to the bridge. At the creek, I wedge myself between slabs of rock, leaning over a spittle of barely flowing creek, scooping water with a ladle. The buckets fill slowly.

Chute Creek is hidden from sight, under a cushion of snow. Today the snow laces the creek, softens the gray rock and buries the water. Buckets filled, I plod back to the house, careful not to slosh the icy water onto my jeans.

❦

February, 1976. 'Finishing' the house involves an endless list of ingredients that still need to be purchased: shelf brackets, shelving materials, wood screws, stain, paint, glue, staples, lighting fixtures, steel wool, irrigation fittings, polyethylene pipe, nails, chisel, sandpaper. These things are essential. The house needs them in order to function.

After another binge at Beaver Lumber, I wonder out loud, "You know, it's like we're retired, spending our days shopping in town."

Jay looks at me as if I'm demented. "But we still have projects to complete!"

I'm worried about money. And I'm tired of being a housewife. "But Jay, we're always buying stuff for the house. We're the ultimate consumers!"

He doesn't get it. He thinks we'll find jobs soon. He says he's been making contacts.

It occurs to me that this is his vocation as well as his avocation. It's my vacation. I like that and repeat it to myself.

❧

The tension gnaws at us. I think of that phrase, "The house is the locus of struggle." Maybe building a house has been a joint venture, but I have become reliant on one man, the only person who can fathom and fix the quirks of the house.

Jay grips the steering wheel while we drive out the Naramata Road.

"I'm sorry," I mumble. "It's just the gender thing." I do not make a good pioneer wife. Women a hundred years ago didn't complain about trips to the hardware store. They were happy to go to town.

But Jay's fed up. "I'm tired of 'the gender thing'. What does it take to make you happy? I've tried just about everything I can think of. I don't know if I can keep this up."

"You?" I explode. "You're like a pig in shit. I'm the odd one out here. Who controls this place? The Regional District, the building code, the fruit co-op – it's all men! Living here is Hockey Night in Canada. Everything happens in a male arena, from hardware to equipment rentals to contractors. Where am I in this picture?"

His shoulders have risen to his chin. "Just because I'm a guy doesn't mean that I control everything! I thought we were in this together, that we were trying to share things more equally."

"Trying doesn't help. That's just not the way things work. You don't understand how lopsided it is, how dependent I am on you. In the city, I'd have a job. There would be other resources! I could take a bus, or call a plumber! It's different for me here than it is for you."

We drive to the house in silence.

View south, early spring.

❦ 10 ❦
Getting Schooled

Summer out here is a nightmare to me. All August was 90° and over. And in this heat
there was fruit picking, jam making and fruit bottling for the winter. Besides all the other
work-but I always seem to be complaining at the poor old jam and it is very grateful
[sic] and comforting to eat when the summer departs ...

DOROTHEA ALLISON. LETTER, 25 SEPTEMBER, 1915

Spring leapfrogs winter with days that explode with sunlight, blossoms and warmth. On the way home from town, I stop in at Eleanor's 'studio', the cabin she has built on top of her cistern, next to the "pottery", jammed with pots, leftover plywood, pieces of kiln, and works in progress. Eleanor is the queen of multi-media.

On the walls, canvasses leaf out in every green – emerald moss, pale sage, chartreuse aspen, bronzed larch, granny-smith apple and the deep dark greens of fir forests. And blue – Mediterranean seas and azure skies, true-blue-blues, sapphire, midnight ... Eleanor stands at the easel, paintbrush in hand, paint streaking her hair and smudging her smock. Colour squishes from tubes onto palettes and walls and the floor.

Tacked on the easel, the view plummets to sun-drenched clay cliffs. Blond hummocks of bunchgrass hills tumble towards the lake. I begin to flip between old canvases and stacked up paintings. It's like being in a candy store! The colours of the entire valley burst from this small space.

I turn back towards the road where Eleanor's goat prances on the hood of my little yellow truck. I dash towards it, flapping my arms and yelling, "Get off, you awful creature!"

This goat is the embodiment of evil. It prances off and away, just as K'tanga, Eleanor's dog, jumps out of the cab of the truck, past me and disappears behind the house. On the passenger seat, the paper sacks from Safeway are tattered. An aluminum foil wrapper lies on the floor. "Damned dog! It's eaten the whole pound of butter!!"

Eleanor stands next to her front porch giggling as the goat prances around the front of the house. "Really, Mel, don't let him get the best of you."

Damn dog, damn goat! She's even talking about getting chickens! In between goddess incarnations, Eleanor spins a current of artwork, as if by spontaneous combustion.

What has happened to my creativity? Did it get lost between the dimensional lumber and the wavy-edged siding?

In May, the machinery of spring works overtime. Buttercups are still in bloom, and spring gold, that lacy yellow lomatium, carrot-tops the dun-colored earth. Saskatoon is budding out. Furry catkins dangle from each aspen branch. Below them, a California quail, with a preposterous top-notch, teeters through the grass like a wind-up toy.

Da Da DAA Da.

Gold bouquets of balsamroot shine on every hillside against old pine needles and the leftover winter. Tiny starflowers pinprick the cream-of-wheat coloured bunchgrass. The ledge in back of the house sparkles with hot-pink shooting stars. I swoon at the front steps, where fleur-de-lis blossoms of saskatoon cascade like honeysuckle over the rocks.

This afternoon I surprise three white-tailed deer. They hold their ground, twitching, muscles tight, while I speak to them in a low voice. Then they bolt uphill, fluffy white tails sweeping back and forth like short feather boas.

Creativity is not an issue here.

❧

Our new friends, James and Bonnie, have come for dinner. They have an orchard in Naramata, two orchards, to be exact. One is a ten-acre block of cherries, 'cots and pears, and the other is apples – Macs, and Red and Golden Delicious, including dwarf trees on trial for the Research Station in Summerland. Before they moved here, James taught political economy at a university. "I wanted to practice what I was teaching. And I couldn't hack the politics of the department any more. I always wanted to farm."

They have three teen-agers. Bonnie chimes in: "We wanted to bring the kids up in a place where they had a connection to the land, so they'd know where food comes from, and how much work it takes to put it on the table."

In addition to making the best apple pie I've ever tasted, Bonnie is an artist. In one of her landscapes, Okanagan Mountain swirls in a bowl of rounded earth and veers towards Squally Point to be swallowed by the lake. Where I see craggy fissures of steel gray ridgelines, Bonnie kneads the mountains so that they rise up like dough.

Tonight, Bonnie's more concerned about the art of everyday life. They're having problems with their road. She spouts, "We couldn't believe it when Arthur blocked our driveway. He said he was going to have to use the road for his machinery."

James chimes in, "He told us, 'Why don't you put up a road around the back of your place?' Then he says, 'The grade's easy, and you can bring it up at the edge of the trees.' "

James shakes his head and takes a breath in between bites. "The next thing we knew, his backhoe was smack in the middle of the drive. Can you believe that? We've been here four-and-a-half years. I thought we were on good terms!"

Bonnie takes over. "It's going to cost us a fortune to put in a new road! It just shows, you never really know about people!"

❦

Tree fruits tie you into the community, human and other. Last week, Alex and Jeannie stopped over for tea, and Alex regaled us with stories about his initiation into the fruit trade.

"I knew nothing about growing fruit, but we moved in next to Paul and Laura Long. Paul helped me through that first year, through the basic sulfur, lime and oil treatment." He pauses.

"In July when I was out in the orchard one day, laying out irrigation pipe, I came across this enormous rattlesnake. I wasn't even wearing my boots. The only protection I had was the pipe. It must have been a twenty-foot run, but I managed to smash the snake with it. So I stretched the snake out on the hood of my truck. I went down to Paul, and asked him to come up and have a look see. I was quite proud, you know. My first Okanagan kill!

"Paul was not pleased. He said, 'Well done, Alex, you've killed a bull snake. This snake would consume hundreds of mice if left to its own devices. We're always happy to have them in the orchard.'"

❦

When I stop in at James and Bonnie's house a week later, she takes me on a walk around their orchard. A patchwork of fruit trees tufts the bench lands like an old chenille bedspread.

"Imagine!" she says, "We consume the fruit of our labour!"

Pink and white apple blossoms polka-dot the trees. "I used to work alone a lot of the time, with the radio for company. Or I'd work with

James. Now we hire out during harvests."

The land rolls around us, lolling uphill to the train tracks and sloping down to gullies, undulating like the supple, living thing that it is. In our gaze, the crops shift to plums, pears and cherries, each block benchmarked by variety, following the lay of the land.

"What about women and farming?" I'm curious. " Do you get credit for doing this, or is it 'housework'?"

She turns away, and looks back uphill. "Well, you know, nobody talks about that. I like the work, and we need the money. But agricultural work is still about men and machines. There's only one woman member. She's Quebecoise, and doesn't come to meetings."

Bonnie scans the hillsides, her gaze tracing the ridgeline north to Okanagan Mountain. "But it's not just that. It's about more than men or women. Sometimes the work is lonely! You worry about the weather. And whether you should tear out the whole orchard and plant grapes, because you can't make a living with fruit trees any more, and the American markets are dumping, and the varieties are changing, and you always have to be ahead of the game."

We're coming back to the house now. She looks at me, and sighs; "More of us are working in town to support family orchards. We're probably the last generation on the land."

Cherries are ripe again, with a forecast of 60 percent probability of precipitation. For orchardists, the June horoscope reads like this: your cherries will be split and un-marketable, the pickers you've lined up will probably vanish into a smog of marijuana and rasta curls or leave for greener pastures, and you'll be picking like a madman for weeks.

Bings, Stellas, Lamberts, Vans – people have surplus cherries or spoiled fruit, so cherries are practically free! We don't have our own trees yet, but we buy a black enamel canning pot, a couple of flats of jars, and a cherry pitter. We pour trainloads of sugar, a taste of almond and a spoon of lemon juice into the mix. Jay pits the cherries and sterilizes and organizes the jars, and I mix the soupy jam, which glurps and bubbles like a volcano. Together, we pour the tacky red glue into glass jars, stick them into the canner, and submerge the whole clanking mess into boiling water.

We've put up a hundred jars of jam. There is sugar everywhere: under my fingernails, under the stove, between the seams of arborite on the kitchen counter. After the smudge of cherry has been sponged from counters, stovetop and floor, rows of small glass jars with bright metal lids line up with military precision.

Jay turns to me, beaming: "Well, that was a lot of work! But it tastes great, and we won't have to worry about Christmas presents this year." He taps a lid, pleased to hear the 'clink' that means there is a vaccuum seal. A regiment of ruby red cut-glass jam jars gleams in the afternoon light.

Putting up fruit converts the kitchen into a factory. I imagine women in long dresses, canning fruit on wood stoves in their summer kitchens, firing up the wood stove on days simmering with heat!

Secretly, I suspect that The Joy of Cooking is hyperbole. The only thing my mother ever 'put up' was birds. Besides, there's always Save-on-Foods.

By mid-July, it's peaches. Jay peels and pits them, cuts sunset-fringed sections and ladles them into the containers, then tops the peaches with syrup. This time we use the quart jars. Dunk! Into the boiling water in the canner. Clink! Onto the counter.

We plant six fruit trees in a patch down the hill, where the soil is deep and the land bowls to suck up the heat. After sinking 12-foot postholes around the perimeter, we string up fencing to keep out deer and bears. We plant two each of apricots, peaches and apples, so they will cross-pollinate.

❦

In early October, I'm on the front porch, watching the rest of the world go by. A cherry-red Cassin's finch warbles an entire opera, while a towhee scuttles in the leaves, wheezing like an emphysema victim. A Clark's nutcracker discovers the circular feeder, jumps on its stick perch, and propels the merry go-round fast forward. Kra-aaa-aaaa! Then he hops to an upper branch and stretches down, glossy black feathers dangling below his trim gray torso like a flamenco dancer. He strains towards the feeder, loses his grip, and flaps down onto the lower branch. The entire sequence repeats itself again and again.

❦

Between freelance writing for Pacific Yachting and Harrowsmith, Jay gets involved in local environmental issues. Over the winter, he and James write The Other Face of 2,4-D to contest the application of phenoxy herbicide 2,4-D to combat the spread of Eurasian water milfoil in the lakes.

Jay is always on the phone. "Can you believe it?" He's talking to his friend Curtis in Naramata. "This class of herbicides was developed as a form of chemical and biological warfare! They used it as a defoliant in Vietnam."

Then he's out the door. "I have a meeting this afternoon in town. I'll be back before dinner."

With dinner, I get a lecture. "This stuff is a known carcinogen and teratogen! The Water Investigations Branch has approved its use, but it's toxic. Now they want to open Skaha Lake when herbicide levels are still high. It hasn't even been absorbed."

But Jay certainly has been!

❧

The next winter I teach a Sociology class at the Penticton branch of Okanagan College. In early May, I see an ad in The Vancouver Sun:

OKANAGAN COLLEGE. FULL-TIME INSTRUCTOR IN SOCIOLOGY.

To teach Sociology 100 (Introduction), Sociology 200 (Theory), Sociology 140 (Canadian Society.) Advanced degree in Sociology required and teaching experience at the post-secondary level advised. Kelowna and Penticton campus, Starts Fall Semester.
Applications must be accompanied by two letters of reference.
Direct inquiries to the Dean of Arts, Okanagan College, 150 KLO Road, Kelowna, B.C.
Final Date of Applications: June 10.

I apply.

❧

I set up an office in Kelowna in September for my new full-time job at Okanagan College. A new colleague who looks like Ward Cleaver introduces himself. "You look like you're new here. I'm Brian Ames. I teach Chemistry here and in Vernon and Salmon Arm."

"Hi Brian. Did you have a good summer?"

"Oh, yes, thanks. We've just come back from the Coast. I spent five weeks in the UBC Library. It gave me a chance to get caught up."

It's not my idea of summer vacation. His wife was probably taking care of the kids.

"So you're getting things set for the term?" I ask.

"I've come to bring in my documents." He sets his bulging brown briefcase on the stairwell, and pulls out a folder. "The librarian at UBC signed me in every day, so that the College would have a record of my attendance."

"Does the College require you to do this? To clock in when you're out of town?" The last time I did that was when I was an undergrad working in food services.

Brian shuffles his feet. "Well, no, not exactly. It's just that I feel better being away for so long when I record my working time."

For this I need an advanced degree?

Mondays and Wednesdays I teach in Kelowna, Tuesdays and Thursdays in Penticton. The drive to Kelowna takes about an hour and a half, sometimes a little more. I wish I could use the direct route, the old KVR track through Chute Lake on the east side of the lake, but its potholes could swallow a car.

My first week of teaching in September 1977, I commute back and forth to Kelowna every other day. I watch as tent caterpillars shred chokecherry leaves into writhing gauze cocoons. I swoon to crimson sumac flares against the blue of the lake. I stop at Antlers Beach south of Peachland to watch for loons and grebes.

After turning into a house/wife, it's hard to face a classroom – much more difficult than carting cement bags or nailing 2 x 4's. But I have a job with a pay cheque and a voice of my own. Teaching Sociology connects me with Canadian society beyond the Okanagan.

I'm thinking about my lecture on Marxist theory as I drive up Drought Hill north of Peachland – how the material conditions of people's lives shape their ideas and activities. For Marx, our beliefs are determined by both the social and physical world in which we live, but especially by our relations to the work we do.

My mind wanders. How does anyone 'belong' to this place anymore? Is home just anywhere you hang your hat? Any place with a pay cheque? How are we attached to a place when we no longer derive our sustenance from it? How do we know what it is? Why should we care?

❦

It's a late October afternoon and Jay and I are out for a hike. As the light fades, the coyotes start to call. Scrambling down the steep bluff at the northern end of our place, we scratch up bones clumped under the crumpled umbrella of last summer's balsamroot.

"Looks like a coyote to me," says Jay. "I think it's the whole skeleton." He hunkers down, his long fingers tracing the basket of the ribcage. It's been picked clean, and it's been there a long time, a gray-blue wash on white. The skull is narrow, with empty eye sockets, and canine teeth.

I can't bring myself to pick it up. These bones belong to the earth, cradled by dust and dry land. "What do you think killed it? How long do you think it's been here?"

Jay just shakes his head. "Probably humans. There used to be bounties on coyotes." He crouches down next to the bones, shaken and subdued.

Tonight the hills ricochet with the yipping of coyotes, sharp and shrill, thin and whimpering; distinct from the whuuffy bark of a domestic dog. Then silence.

A minute later the siren starts again, shrill and high, a keening like something in pain. Tiny sharp yips pinch the night and send shivers up my spine.

❦

Full-time post-secondary education means two semesters, night and day classes, lectures and examinations; conferences and course development and research: abstract ideas, printed words, spoken words, papers, books, words, and more words. You can't eat it, but the pay cheque is dependable and the work is portable.

Perhaps too portable. I commute back and forth between the Penticton and Kelowna campuses, and rent a cottage in downtown Kelowna so that I don't have to drive the whole distance every day, especially after night classes in the winter.

I still know little about the day-to-day livelihood of agriculture. The natural subsidiary of B.C. Tree Fruits – saskatoon, crabapples, pin cherries, Oregon grape, thimbleberries, and black-capped raspberries – is more familiar to me than its commercial varieties. The production, distribution, and marketing of fruit, its subsidies, labour, global competition and environmental externalities remain material for future research.

I have learned this: the agricultural year involves a sequence that includes planning, grafting, planting, pruning, fertilizing, spraying, pruning, thinning, fertilizing, harvesting, pruning ... And this: seasons and the market drive orchard work. In winter, even when the trees are dormant, your fingers burn from pruning in the cold. The work never stops.

There are more jobs like mine as the Okanagan shifts from a resource economy with an agricultural focus to a service economy. Even with the creation of the Agricultural Land Reserve in 1973, more than a quarter of Valley farmland will be converted to non-agricultural use over the next fifteen years. Vineyards and wineries have already begun to replace orchards. It's not just me. The entire Valley is in transition.

❦

In 1977, Penticton classes at Okanagan College are held in a former Catholic school with square rooms, straight rows of desks, blackboards and lectern – designed to convey doctrine and authority. But sometimes I think I'm the one who's getting schooled.

"I had a dream about you last night," chuckles Harry, as I drag my briefcase into the office. His big blue eyes sparkle as he licks his lips and gives me a wink.

Maybe the convent is a cover for Sin City! Harry becomes my favorite colleague in Penticton – articulate, critical, witty and bright. At least he talks to me! Other faculty members are more aloof. I am the only regular female academic instructor at the Penticton branch of the College.

My friend Joan, who teaches at the College in Kamloops, was told by a colleague: "You've taken a job that would support an entire family."

"The Okanagan is a great place to bring up a family." People say that.

Journal Entry, December 1977

I yoyo to Kelowna and back again every other day to teach. Tonight is Monday night, the first week in December, and we've already had our first snow. I've taught two classes in Kelowna, and I'm coming home to Naramata tonight to teach in Penticton tomorrow. I drive slowly as I get out to our end of the road, because the road is icy. As I turn off the dirt road and across the field, my tires are spinning out.

I weasel under the car to put on the chains. The headlights funnel ahead into the pine trees. In the dark behind them, I stick a flashlight in the snow so I can see the links of chain. My knee-high boots and jumper and tights snowball beneath my jacket, damp and frozen. My gloves are wet. Except for the clink of my fumbling efforts with the chains, the night is cold and dark and still. As I tie the last links, a great horned owl calls out of the stark black and white of the snowy night:

"Whooo, oo, ooo. Whoo, oo, ooo."

I jump to my feet, brush the snow from my legs, and scan the trees. There is no sign of the owl.

"Whooo, oo, ooo. Whoo, oo, ooo."

Who are you, and what are you doing here?

❦ 11 ❦
The Way Out

My father was an Oxford man, and entirely unsuited to pioneer life …
He never would have pioneered at all, except that my mother was of the
adventurous type, who felt the urge to go west. She liked it very much and she was very,
very brave about it; but she felt, inwardly, that she had been defeated in her idea.
I mean, it was not what she thought it was going to be.

R.J. SUGARS, IN BRIGHT SUNSHINE AND A BRAND NEW COUNTRY

In January 1979, my second year teaching at the College, the little house I've rented in Kelowna is colder than a meat locker. Water pipes are frozen all over town. The first day of the new semester, I inform my class, "I wanted to give you the news myself. I'm pregnant. The baby is due after the end of the term, in May, so there won't be any interruption with classes."

I'm wearing my big, billowing purple smock. "Attention, Sociology 100!" I might have announced. "Your class this term will be taught by an eggplant." Pregnancy inevitably becomes public domain, an act of personal exposure. Over the next three months, at least twenty-five people tell me, "Having a baby will change your life."

That's why I'm pregnant.

❦

I finish the Caribou Marathon with a respectable time: 6 months pregnant, with a 7-hour finish, and 200 trips "to the ladies' room" (except
there aren't any.) The 'ladies room' consists of around-the-snowbank
stops and furtive behind-the-aspen-grove forays, and off-the-course-and-
around-the-corner breaks, and Jay-trying-to-shelter-me-but-I-don't-care-
anymore old-fashioned stops. I should be skiing in a skirt.

A month later we ski backcountry with friends near Lake Louise,
bunking in the Mosquito Creek hostel, up to its armpits in snow. Skiing
back to the cabin one day I tumble upside down into the powder of a
tree well. Snow drifts down over my blue sweater and around the lake of
my blimp belly. I can't even move until Tom M. comes back to hoist me
out. When John gets up at 4:30 in the morning to start the fire, I'm
already training for post partum.

Two weeks after I submit my grades, the Clivus Multrum toilet is
baptized with amniotic fluid. At dawn's light, Jay and I shuffle out the
path and bounce downhill in the truck. We pogo downhill past indiffer-
ent mule deer, then chant Lamaze mantras on the Grand Prix into town.
Four days later Phoebe and I lie on the porch in the early summer sun,
her big brown eyes fixed on aspen branches that flutter with new leaves
and light.

❦

Jane Goodwin, a friend of Jay's from the South Okanagan Environmental
Coalition, is on the phone. "Isn't it amazing how natural it is to be a
mother? Nobody has to tell you what to do; you just know."

That's it! I call for Jay and jam the phone into his hand, then lace up
my runners, make sure Phoebe is asleep, and dash out of the house. I
run up the hill, down the road, across the bridge past Eleanor's, over
Harrises' Road to Mandalay to the main dirt road, out to Hunt's pond

and down to the old dump. I stagger to a sweaty walk before I turn back uphill, back to my new night-and-day job – the relentless on-call duty of childcare. Crybaby nights I pad back and forth in the living room, looking beyond the dark surrounds of the house to the shimmer of Summerland across the lake. They say that ninety percent of the universe is composed of dark matter. That sounds about right.

It's come down to nurture versus nature. Sociologists emphasize the cultural determinants of child rearing over the biological. I am desperate for daycare, child support, and friends with babies. Right now, nature seems to be winning.

❦

Nature wins again with the annual Nest Record count. This is the first time we've been active participants in the nesting activity. This time when the alarm goes off in the back of the truck, it takes half an hour to get dressed and change Phoebe (who has been up most of the night.)

"We're behind schedule. It's already starting to get light." Jay is fumbling with the counting records and the binoculars. "Let's get moving. You can feed her while we're driving."

This time Jay does the timing, listening, identification, counting, and the driving. I'm with Phoebe. "I'm pretty sure that's waxwings over there, that wispy sound. And these are kinglets up here." Jay nods at the big lodgepole pine on the other side of the road.

Phoebe is doing her normal call: "Wahhh, Waaaahh, WAAAHHH." I rock her, bump her up and down and cuddle her.

It's light. So far, I've counted about ten birds, including robins, Clark's nutcrackers, and pygmy nuthatches and an osprey. We're coming out onto the grasslands in back of Princeton to pothole lakes dimpled with ducks. Phoebe is finally asleep. When we stop for the last count, we leave the engine on to keep her quiet.

That's our last nest records count.

Phoebe is about six weeks old when we're out to survey the morning with our friends Rob and Joanne. Rob totes Phoebe, who yammers away from her backpack perch, playing with his ponytail. Coming home, he strides ahead, probably planning afternoon chores as he disappears around the corner of the path towards the house.

"Fire! FIRE!! Hurry it up, guys!" Robbie yells from the front porch.

When we get there, Phoebe wails from her backpack, which is opened like a sandwich board on the front porch. Straddling the front door sill, fire extinguisher in hand, Robbie pitches things outside and onto the porch. Inside, shaving cream lines of white foam dribble across the heater like hot cross buns. Thunderclouds of smoke pour out the door.

"What did you leave here? It's stuck to the heater like plastic." Robbie is frantically opening the windows inside to clear the smoke. Jay races inside the house to help.

It smells like a chemical factory.

"Diapers." I'm jiggling Phoebe in my arms, trying to recall. " I think I left a diaper on top. But, we haven't used the heater for hours. Not since first thing this morning when I was burning some trash."

"It was still hot enough to burn diapers," spurts Rob, breaking through the front door for a breather, "And look!" He points over to the curtains, peppered with singed bullet holes from the sparks. "If we hadn't come back right now, they would have gone up."

Jay snuggles Phoebe, rocking her back and forth to quiet her down. "We could have lost the whole thing," he whispers to her. "Just like that!"

At two months, Phoebe is hiking Lake O'Hara, gurgling at hikers and mountains from her pack. She backpacks with us at Yoho National Park, where we camp precariously on the Whaleback, a monolithic rock over-looking the valley. If our own little pika could crawl, we wouldn't be up here.

On the Road, we're fine. But once we're home, the Subterranean Dharma Blues wash over me again. When I was a teen-ager, I wanted to be a beatnik. I hung out in coffee houses, read City Lights, and idolized Ginsberg and Kerouac's rants and travels and freedom. But that was the 50's. That was before consciousness-raising.

What did Jack Kerouac know, anyhow? He was a guy.

❦

We've passed the honeymoon period. And so, it seems, has everyone else. Every community experiences conflict, but lately, everyone seems to be squabbling:

James and Bonnie have lost their road access;

The Ranch has notified the neighbours about 'trespassing';

Johnsons have cut off Matt and Suzanne's water access;

Chapman's cows are running all over the place;

Meanes' powerboat throbs louder than Chute Creek Falls in full flood;

So this isn't Happy Valley. I know that. When we moved here, we enjoyed a détente. There were fewer demands on roads and water, and lots of camaraderie, not to mention endless help from our neighbours.

But beneath the surface, there have been conflicts. The dispute may be nothing significant, but the edges of the place become a little rougher over time. Any human society includes cooperation as well as conflict, but in a small community all interaction is personalized. The webs and the splits become lessons in the geography of place.

Neutrality is a myth.

❦

Chute Creek is the signature of this place and an antidote to the currents of human strife. The turbulence of water in the creek is a measure of season and gradient. The spring creek boils, bubbles and rackets in turmoil, too agitated to be 'white' water. At full force, when the creek squirts from the cliff face, I think about the boy with his finger in the dyke, and wonder if spring run-off could explode the mountainside.

Even then the creek is camouflaged with mock orange, dogwood and willows, cloaking the water's flow. By August it will be thinned by the demands of irrigation and upstream use to trickle like an I.V. through this dry sparse place where nothing seems alive. After the leaves drop and the pipes are shut down for the winter, Chute Creek re-emerges. In November, crystals form along the edges of creek bed, the ice moving in as the water bubbles underneath.

And then it will be spring again and the entire rocky cliff will drip and rain with splashing water. Fragile ferns will unfurl from crevices of rock. The musty, dank smell of freshwater creek will drift over the falls and drizzle into mist like a coast swathed in fog.

When I drive to town, I listen to CBC. One day I listen to a call-in show about investments in stocks and mutual funds.

"Calculate strategies for dumping; don't wait until you are forced to sell," says the expert. I try to translate this into familiar territory. What about life investments: friends, work and place? How can you calculate personal investments in market terms?

"You always need an exit strategy," says the expert.

An ancient ponderosa pine, *pinus ponderosa* stands in front of the house, contorted but statuesque. Its patchy, popeye arms sweep the inertia of early afternoon. Twig-stumped branches prickle in the heat; needles sift the evening breeze. The tree grows from glacial-scoured granite, which explains its dwarfed height and the twists and turns of trunk and branches. Its bonsai roots tunnel through rock, seeking pockets of soil.

Suspended between rock and sky, the tree scratches out a subsistence living. Beetles or drought threaten many yellow pines in the valley. Beneath their patchwork puzzles, bark beetle larvae burrow into wood in home invasions unreported by the Penticton Herald.

This tree candelabras lake and sky; it precedes and may outlive me. It is quiet against my noise. It knows how to hold on.

❦

Right now all I'm holding is Phoebe. I feel like I'm in an earthquake, teetering on the brink of marriage. The bedrock is crumbling.

Jay paces back and forth in the kitchen. "I know we can work it out. We're not the first people in history to have a baby in the boonies. There's probably good day care in Penticton if we want. As good as Vancouver. And if you want to keep your job, I'm here for Phoebe. Any time. All the time."

The dry branches of saskatoon scratch at the front porch in the evening breeze. The plateau is parched.

My voice shakes. "Are you kidding? You can say that you're here for her. But I won't be. I'll be commuting to Kelowna and back. How can I do that with a baby?"

Phoebe starts to whimper, and Jay picks her up, swings her gently through the air. "You can quit your job. I can get work in town."

"Yes, but I want to work. I don't want to have to worry about your pay cheque. And I need my own identity. I want to be something besides a mom."

Phoebe's still fussing.

"Maybe she's hungry," says Jay, handing Phoebe back to me. "We can live here on a fraction of our former budget."

I jiggle her in my lap. I'm too upset to feed her. "I don't want to worry about money," I urge, my voice rising. "Some day I'm going to want to wear something besides workboots and my wool jacket. And Phoebe will need things."

I'm looking out the front window. The lake pools to the south as lights twinkle on in Penticton. "The baby changes things," I say into the dusky evening. "I don't want to raise a baby where we have to drive to get everything - babysitters, friends, food..."

The floodgates open, and I'm sobbing. Phoebe is crying. I continue. "This place is beautiful, but we've retired too soon. We're too young to be here. Practically everyone is older than us. We're out of synch."

I can't stop. "Having Phoebe makes all that clear. It's too hard. I want my life back. Movies, friends my age, work, running water, a sidewalk, front steps."

"Hey, we've got front steps!" Jay is trying to lighten things up.

"You don't get it!" I stop and blow my nose.

🦌

Phoebe's still sniffling. "That's not all!" I add. "I've stopped seeing the place. We might as well be living in Mississauga, or Burnaby, or Levittown."

Jay doesn't answer. Then he states slowly, "Maybe that means we're really home. Maybe it's only exotic and beautiful and endangered when you're a tourist. If it's home, you take it for granted, like the people who live with you."

Outside, the light has faded, and bats flutter around the open porch. Above the lake, a nighthawk plummets in the groan of freefall. Phoebe fidgets with my keys – her favorite toy. I look at Jay, his shoulders hunched up to his earlobes, bent over the kitchen counter like an old man. He hates to argue.

He pauses, then slowly straightens up and takes a deep breath. He walks across the kitchen towards me and swoops Phoebe into the air, leaning over to give me a long kiss. "All right," he says, with finality. " Let's go to the city for a year and rent a place. You can go back to school, and I'll get a job. We'll keep this place, and when we're ready, we'll be back. The place will wait."

There is nothing left to say.

The view south.

Sagebrush Mariposa Lily, *Calochortus macrocarpus*.

PART THREE
Homecoming

When I think of these times, and call back to my mind the grandeur and beauty of those almost uninhabited shores ... when I reflect that all this ..., instead of being in a state of nature, is now more or less covered with villages, farms, and towns. .. when I remember that these extraordinary changes have all taken place in the short period of twenty years, I pause, wonder, and ... can scarcely believe its reality.

– JOHN JAMES AUDUBON, "THE OHIO,"
ORNITHOLOGICAL BIOGRAPHY, 1831-1839

❦ 12 ❦
Endgame

The record of a country's history is not only... of great and grand events. ... it is
the details of the lives of ordinary people and day to day events that complete the picture
and give it meaning. Too often it is these details, so fundamental to the life of a nation,
which go unwritten and become lost in the mists of time.

– H. HERRIDGE, IN ATKINSON, "EARLY PENTICTON," OKANAGAN HISTORY

We leave the Granite Farm on Labour Day. Phoebe natters herself to sleep
in the car, but Jay and I simmer in silence. We're deportees of our own
idealism – a post-urban neo-ruralism whose challenges I have failed. I
feel selfish and neglectful, as if I'm responsible for the abandonment of
our dreams.

"We'll build a sweet little nest, somewhere in the West," has turned
out to be an anachronism, a construct of rugged individualism. Sure,
gender equality and a biocentric land ethic remain compelling concepts.
But theory is different from praxis, whether it's the preservation of land
or marriage. It's difficult to implement these ideas in an existing context, whether marriage, community or market economies.

Sure, Jay and I resisted the domestication of the Granite Farm, but
our activity has had its impacts. We may not have farmed a crop, but our
'ecologically sensitive' home consumes energy and converts natural habi-

tat. Even using a pick-and-shovel as a front-end loader, we've been a part of the unraveling of place, the deconstruction of nature. We are complicit in the fragmentation of the valley, the province, and North America.

I consider this as we drive through Olalla and into Keremeos, where the steep slopes of K and Chopaka mountains shunt us into the Cascades. Abandoned mining cabins, testament to the dreams of an earlier generation, trace the Similkameen west on the Crowsnest Highway.

I think about the movement of humans through exploration, resource extraction, nation building, market expansion and war. The outcomes of human encroachment on places like this are varied but cumulative – the colonization of landscape, the appropriation of carrying capacity, and the subversion of natural systems to the needs and desire of the human species.

Our move to the city is a short and voluntary migration. It pales in comparison to that of early settlers - the icy winds of winter prairie crossings, trains of wartime migrants, ships and busloads of immigrants, diasporas of the persecuted, the endless migration of human beings on this planet, push-pulled by politics, religion, desperation, and the promise of better lives.

I am already homesick.

❦

In the city, Phoebe is in daycare with a family that has adopted all of us, while I'm back working on my degree at UBC and Jay works at SPEC, an environmental organization. Back in Naramata for the summer, I trade baby-sitting twice a week with Jennifer, who also has a one-year old. I don't make much progress on my thesis.

Today I pick up the mail at the rural delivery site, where bluebirds flit back and forth from willows to fencepost perches. A large manila envelope awaits me, with feedback on Chapter One from Jasper McMahon, one of my committee members. I tear open the envelope. A bloodline of red ink scribbles over and under every line, as if scrawled by a madman. Whirligig words spill over and under the lines, into the margins and through the sentences. I can barely decipher his comments. At the bottom of page 4, Jasper has written, "You get the drift ..."

The "drift" prompts a flood of nausea. It's not just what he's said; it's how he's said it, slashing every one of my words in a pen-and-ink massacre. On a bright Okanagan summer day, while bluebirds twitter over the Naramata Road, I have been crushed. This man has rejected all of my ideas and put me in my place.

But I am already in my place. Yes, Rural Route One is a combat zone of property rights, apple markets, coddling-moth invasions, water rights, and making-ends-meet. Living in a rural community isn't easy, but at least I'm grounded. The petty politics of thesis committees, supervisory rejection and the hierarchy of the academy no longer defeat me. I stick the pages back in the envelope and head back out the winding road to our log house.

Another year passes, and I'm still working on my Ph.D. I've changed advisors and committee members, and written hundreds of pages, but progress is slow. I'm still on leave from Okanagan College. The next year I'm pregnant again. There's no going back. I give notice to the College.

And I resign from the Granite Farm.

Jay has adjusted to staying in Vancouver. "The Granite Farm will wait until we get back. The systems are resilient, so we don't need to be there all the time. We both have jobs, so we can afford to stay here as long as we need."

I'm feeling guilty. Not enough to move back to the Granite Farm with two small children. It's like I've turned my back on something, abdicated my responsibility.

❧

Time flies; things change. Home is where you can make a living. Over the next two decades I teach Sociology in Vancouver at various colleges and universities; Jay works in different jobs; the kids are in school. We skip town to the Granite Farm for long weekends and summer vacations, trying to hold on. The fruit trees in the garden succumb to heat and lack of water; the scrawny aspens around the house barely survive the summer heat.

One spring Vancouver evening during the calamity of bedtime, Jay answers the phone to hear a familiar, lilting voice. "Jay, it's Eleanor. I'm calling to let you know that the creek is in full flood. Your bridge is in danger."

Jay is on alert! "How high is the water, Eleanor?"

He doesn't wait for her to answer. " How did this happen? Should I come up?" He is ready to go.

We haven't been there for spring runoff for several years. Eleanor replies with care, "I'm not sure whether the creek has peaked. It's very high this year. You know they've been logging up at Chute Lake ..."

Jay begins to reply, but Eleanor continues. "Just now there are several large pieces of timber stuck uphill of the bridge, in a log jam, so the creek's flowing in the secondary channel." That means that the creek already spans a twenty-foot run.

Next morning, Jay is on his way. He calls me that afternoon. "By the time I got here, the bridge was already starting to go. Some big timbers got hung up, and the water rose until it floated up around the bridge, and washed away the supports."

His voice breaks. "There was nothing I could do."

❧

Jay builds a footbridge across the creek. Now we cross the bridge on foot and lug our stuff up the remaining road to our former parking lot. It's not just the bridge; we're starting to lose our grip on the place. We dash to the Granite Farm every chance we get, but we can't keep up with basic maintenance.

They say 'nature abhors a vacuum', and the basic principles of ecological succession prove true – weeds are growing everywhere, especially in 'disturbed' areas. A weed is a plant that grows where people do not want it.

An unwanted plant is a noxious weed. This year, the hills are massed with (1) candles of mullein, (2) knapweed, prickly and stiff, which invades the road, and (3) sweet clover seven feet tall! '"Les mauvaises herbes" ripple into the valley - louche, untamable, rebellious, and decadent - a menace. Instead of my plant identification book, I need a weed primer.

SOME WEEDS OF THE GRANITE FARM:

Diffuse Knapweed:	(Centaurea diffusa)
Spotted Knapweed:	(Centaurea maculosa)
Great Mullein:	(Verbascum thapsus)
Yellow Salsify:	(Tragopogon dubius)
Perennial Sow-Thistle:	(Sonchus arvensis)
Sweet clover:	(Melilotus alba)
Quackgrass:	(Agropyron repens)
Foxtail barley:	(Hordeum jubatum)
Cheatgrass:	(Bromus tectorum)
Sheep sorrel:	(Rumex acetosella)
Poison Ivy:	(Rhus radicans)
Dalmatian Toadflax	(Linaria genistifolia ssp. dalmatica)
Humans	(Homo Sapiens)

Obnoxious weeds! They harbour insects and disease, compete with agricultural crops; and require great expense to control. Weeds are an eyesore; they depreciate land values. Crop loss due to weeds amounts to millions of dollars. Weeds are opportunistic; they invade and succeed, often in a silent takeover by unbidden upstarts; they have the makings of dominion.

While Phoebe and Gabe have afternoon naps, I pull up (4) salsify plants. I expand to (5) cheat grass, which siphons spring water from natural grasses and plants, and even more (6) knapweed, because once you get it on your hands, its bitterness contaminates everything you touch, like bad medicine. I know that the soil disruption from my efforts is the foundation for additional weeds, but left untouched, these plants will go to seed. Around me, geodesic domes of salsify seed heads parachute through the air.

One summer, Jay builds a tree house in the gully in back of the house, "to keep the kids happy." It's out of sight, tucked among a few Douglas firs, small and cozy, perfect for children.

"Why don't you kids go down there and spend the night?" Jay prompts. But nobody ever does.

"Dad, maybe we'll just sleep on the front porch."

Maybe cactus, rats, rattlers and bears are a factor. These are children of the Coast. This place is our adventure, not theirs.

A few years later, I walk down the draw behind the house. The tree house hangs at an angle just above the ground, listing heavily to starboard. I climb down to check it out. Its sailing days are over. The yawing of trees during winter storms has worked the spikes loose; it careens ungracefully towards the earth.

Jay levels it with concrete blocks and a block and tackle. Now it's a tiny cabin under the trees. The kids never notice.

Time passes like this.

❦

The nuclear family with teen-aged kids hangs out on the front porch on a lazy summer evening. By the 1990's, our visits are an exercise in seclusion. We haven't kept in contact with local families.

"Why didn't you buy land up the coast? Why did you move here?" Gabe asks. A few of his friends have cabins on Texada or Lasqueti.

"Well..." I reply. "It was too expensive to buy land on the water. And too rainy to stay on the coast."

"But this?" he scans the burned out bunchgrass in front of the cabin, the splintered, sagging porch railings. "It's way too hot to live here." His friends don't want to come any more. They're bored with water slides and mini-golf.

Phoebe chimes in. "And it's too long to come for a weekend."

"We didn't move here for a weekend. This isn't a summer place! We moved here for good."

❦

JOURNAL ENTRY, SUMMER, 1994.

At the water slide just north of Skaha Lake, the kids and I slip down plastic tubes, swathed in sunscreen and chlorinated water, while above us, the Garnet fire rages. It has already destroyed 18 houses and evacuated thousands of people. Smoke hangs in the air like a heavy fog, with a ragged, throat-burning taste that clings to you, that doesn't wash off, even in turquoise tunnels of bliss.

The Word: Ministry of Forests: Henceforth, fire suppression efforts will be replaced by prescribed burns, to minimize fuel load accumulation and restrict the extent and frequency of possible conflagration.

The Subtext: The ponderosa just outside the front door is understoried by a century of history: mattresses of pine needles and duff, snags, fallen branches, pinecones, and decaying logs. Our new address is: the "forest-human interface."

❧

The next year, breaking news arrives in the mail:

This is to inform you that as of April 25, 1995, a gate will be installed for the management of cattle and kept locked to protect livestock. We suggest that you contact the owners to secure provision for access. You will be required to provide specific information concerning times and dates of passage through this point of access.

"I can't believe this. How could anyone do this?" Jay looks like he's opened a letter bomb.

He jumps to his feet, waving the letter in his hand. "But Everett wrote an access into our sales agreement! He promised us to make it legal. They're cutting off our access!"

We've lost another round.

Chute Creek Falls.

❦ 13 ❦
Access

As the valley was divided into small farms and orchards, most of the large ranches soon disappeared. With their passing, a way of life also ended ... characterized by the importance of a man's handshake or his word.

– R.J. SUGARS, IN BRIGHT SUNSHINE AND A BRAND NEW COUNTRY

When we moved here, the land was an empire of bunchgrass. Sagebrush hills and grass-riddled benchlands stretched from our place all the way across the horizon, from the rock ridgeline under Okanagan Mountain south to the railway line. The land flowed like the sea. You could get lost in it.

Bit by bit, fences chopped the landscape into subdivisions and orchards, pasture and vineyards, fragmented and subjugated to human use. When we purchased the steep land on the northern fringe of Harrises, we assumed an entitlement founded on word, nuance, and better times, on a friendship attenuated by shifting relationships, market values and the passing of time. .

❦

Losing our road access feels like someone has died. Jay and I roller coaster through the Kubler-Ross model of loss: shock, hurt, anger, depression, disbelief, hurt, denial, thumb-sucking, hurt, anger, depression, all over again.

Perhaps beauty is enough. High above Okanagan Lake, tiny bolts of colour dart between clumps of sage and straggling antelope brush. Blue larkspur, magenta shooting stars, and the creamy froth of death camas will soon be smothered by blankets of heat. Two months from now, this bare-boned earth will be bleached and brittle, the leaves of sagebrush curled to lick the sky for rain.

Closer to earth, milky pink blooms of rockrose float above lichened granite. Bitterroot. Boiled and eaten by indigenous peoples, its roots extend into crevices in the rock, where they source the moisture of seasons past. This plant comes from nowhere. Next week it will be gone, crumpled by ray-gun sun and thirsty soil, to wait and reappear next spring. Lewisia rediviva. Back to life.

❦

The middle-aged couple wonders what to do. They stand in front of the house, the land falling away at their feet. It's too steep for a road. Anywhere else this would be spring, with soft breezes blowing up the lake, green shoots slivering into clumps of bunchgrass, and tiny knots of aspens in early leaf.

Against the engine drone of waterfall, he states slowly, as if the words are thinking for him, "We could go to court, because access is granted in the Sales Agreement. And we've had continuous road access until now."

Pacing back and forth in front of the house, he stutters: "But even if we win! It would be like driving through a minefield."

She walks out to the edge of the plateau and scans down the waterfall, where the clatter of rockfall plunges into bunchgrass. Perhaps you could thread a road up from the bottom along the creek and through the small pillows of benchland, but once you reach the waterfall, it's too steep.

Maybe a path could work from there, she thinks, trying to trace a route. "We're not finished yet. Remember how we built this place?" she muses out loud.

He walks over next to her, and peers downhill, tracing the escarpment through outcrops of granite into sandy soil, and down into the clay hillsides that border the paved road.

❦

We string a line from the main road up towards the house. Pink double-bubble flagging tape festoons shrubs, dangles from boughs of yellow pine, and dances up the draw into rockier terrain. At the bottom of the waterfall, where the hillside steepens, the ribbon ties onto a branch of saskatoon. That's the end of the road. From here you proceed uphill by foot.

A few weeks later, Jay heads up from Vancouver to work on the road with our neighbour Tom and his bulldozer. The next morning he phones down to the city, in a state of euphoria. "It's finished!"

In the land of gridlock, the kids have already left for school. I'm getting ready to drive to the College, where I teach Society and Environment in a classroom without windows, to students who live in a city where even the colour green is artificial.

"What's finished?"

"The road!" Jay is gleeful.

"But I thought it would take days," I say, throwing my lectures into a folder.

"So did I!" he exclaims. "I woke up early, ran down the hill, and Tom was already there. He drove his tractor up, set the blade and was ready to roll. We made a loop for the car up at the top, and then he just munched his way downhill."

He is charged up, like in the old days. "In two hours, he ran a road from the falls to the main road. Tom really knows how to move that thing!"

"That's great, honey. But I've got to go." I hang up, set the security alarm, and shoulder the front door open, briefcase stuffed with books and papers. My purse is slung around my neck, jacket bunched over my arm. I am late for class, and it's an hour's drive to work.

Below Marine Drive, which takes me to the college in New Westminster, the Fraser River rides bareback to the sea, roiling with industrial effluent, agricultural runoff and heartland precipitate. Back eddies of upstream debris thicken with silt and salmon and perhaps the last sturgeon. I think about the back-and-forth of driving to work every day, how watersheds are choked by new bridges to suburbs and jobs, and how driving to the Okanagan is just a commute on a larger scale. It's mid-morning, so the traffic is light as I turn onto Granville Street. There! Mount Baker snowcones the southeast horizon.

Then I remember to breathe.

TRANSPORTATION INVENTORY: COMING AND GOING

1800's: Hudson Bay Fur Brigade Trail (Horses, Footpaths)

1892: C.P.R. service - Penticton and Okanagan Landing (Paddle wheeler)

1915: Kettle Valley Railway (Steam locomotive)

1949: Completion of Hope-Princeton Highway from Vancouver (Automobile)

1958: Kelowna floating bridge replaces ferry (Vehicular traffic)

1974: Short path out to the Granite Farm house from logging road (Foot. Tractor)

1990: Coquihalla Highway completed

1995: New dirt track uphill from paved road to falls (4-wheel drive)

2008: New Kelowna bridge opened

Continuing: Switchback path to house (Footpath)

Progress!

Thirty years after we started this project, we're building another path to the house. The hillside is too steep to put in a road or use machinery. Progress is slow and sporadic. I wedge big rocks and boulders out of place with the prybar and slide them into place below the path. Sometimes they break loose and tumble downhill. I think of men carving the Hudson's Bay Brigade Trail through the Cascades and the rock-crushing work of building the Kettle Valley Railway. I get dizzy when I look up - at the old road skirting the bank above me, the waterfall thundering downhill, the crumbling hillside, and the car glinting below - the forces of time and gravity.

I'm paying the price. Around me, ponderosa pines giraffe into the sky, and the waterfall dribbles in mid-summer lassitude. The small of my back is large with pain. I'm covered with dirt, which trickles down over the top of my boots, and drifts over my body as suspended solids, grains of sand and dust.

Twenty years ago, a small tractor could make it out to the house from the parking lot. Nowadays we carry everything up and down to the house by hand - food, drinking water, and supplies. This is not progress!

Jay muscles our new hand-me down stove and washing machine up the steep path with a fridge dolly. But when he carts the old washing machine downhill, the old washer whips out of his hands at the last switchback, rolls end-for-end, and finally skids to a halt.

"Must be the spin cycle," he chortles, struggling to lever the rusty washer to an upright position.

❧ 14 ❧
Falling Waters

The water resources... are now heavily licensed, primarily for agriculture and domestic water supply...The demand for water continues to increase. ... population is now {2005} nearly triple what it was in 1974.... in the future summers will tend to be longer, warmer, and drier than they are now...The result will be increasing demand with a decreasing supply of water...If these trends continue, the economic and environmental well being of the Okanagan basin will be seriously threatened within the next several decades.

– CANADIAN WATER RESOURCES ASSOCIATION.
WATER – OUR LIMITING RESOURCE

During the summer, I'm at the Granite Farm by myself. Every morning I turn on the valve in the basement to start the irrigation around the house. If I'm lucky, water spurts through the pipes with a shrill pitch as if it's ready to burst. Several times a day I move the hoses, watching for rattlers, which are attracted to water like all living things.

If I can't get the water running, I'll go to the cistern above the house and carefully reach my gloved hand into the junction box, where wasps have taken up residence. I'll change the valves to close the creek run and open the cistern. I'll be frugal with this water. Living here has taught me the basics - water is essential to life but it comes from somewhere else and does not always bend to need or desire.

❧

The place is parched. When I drive up our road, a posse of dust devils chases the car in hot pursuit. On the turns, the road turns to silt and the car is engulfed in clouds of dust. The water in the creek is so low that the system airlocks. I stumble up and down the creekbed, tramp under alder and dappled birch, and lurch over fallen branches, opening all the valves.

Then I slide down the bank above the water intake, pry off my hiking boots, and edge my legs into the creek. This pool is ice-cold, furry with silt and golden as leopard skin in the dappled sunlight. As my bare feet cloud over with creek muck, I run my hands along the drilled PVC head and start to pump.

I only have the strength for fifty or so pumps at a time. In between, I pause, scanning the creek bed for bears. The foliage is thick and shrubby down here, just the place for a dark feral body on a hot day. When my arm burns from fatigue, I wiggle the head back onto the pipe, holding it under water, waiting for a murmur against my fingers, like checking out the vacuum cleaner hose for suction.

There is nothing.

❧

Jay drives up the next weekend to jump-start the water. He flies out of the house, clutching the plastic pool pump, screwdriver and a pocketful of hose fittings. In thirty minutes, the faucets throb and the outdoor sprinklers thrash as water spurts through the pipe again. He stomps back into the house, dirt-smeared and sweaty.

"This should last for a while," he says, grinning as he clunks across the floor in his workboots, leaving a trail of dust and dirt.

❧

We drive north to Armstrong, where Eleanor now lives. She is launching a retrospective of her work for her 80th birthday. I tell her about our new road and my problems with water, and pass on the latest neighborhood gossip. She commiserates, her long russet hair drifting down her back. A translucent botanical outfit wafts over her tall lithe frame – our guru goddess, First Lady of Stonecrop.

"You know, I can't go back..." Eleanor swirls her teaspoon in the glass.

"Yes, I know." I would give anything to have her back.

"I look back on it now and I think about all the time I lost bickering and worrying. It wasn't that way at first. But the last ten years...There was too much time wasted in trying to hang on," Eleanor sighs.

She reaches over and puts her arm around me. "You have to move on. You already did. You were the first to go, after all."

Just up the logging road lies an old piece of spring-coiled wooden flume that was used to irrigate Paradise Ranch before the advent of PVC pipe. These days, irrigation lines from creeks and lakes supply fruit trees, grape-vines, homestead lilacs and field-grown tomatoes. The aridity of this region, with less than twelve inches a year annual rainfall, makes water a primary concern The entire valley drips, spurts and pulses, hooked up to life support.

From the front porch, the lake glimmers like a mirage. It's hard to imagine current in this pool, to find the old meanders between the lakes, or to trace the south-bound flow of the Okanagan watershed to the Columbia. From here the lake looks landlocked, but it has ambition: to filter from this dry interior into coastal forests, to wash into the Pacific in another climate, another country.

The next day we're at the Naramata Store when we run into Dan Harris, who has moved into Eleanor's cabin with his wife and kids. He and Jay discuss the spring ritual of cistern clean up. Or maybe they're talking pest management?

Jay laughs. "This has been a very good year. Only three rats and eight mice in the cistern! They were so mushy, I just bucketed them out." *Bucketed?*

Dan shakes his head. "Yeah, but if you get a good siphon going, they're easy to clean out." *Siphoned?*

Jay nods his head up and down in agreement. "You've got a two inch pipe. That must really suck." *Suck?*

Dan is into the game. "Yeah, mine can suck marmots. What can yours do?"

Jay laughs. "Mine's good for fish, chipmunks and mice."

Later that day, I trudge up to the empty cistern to take Jay a sandwich. I peer down into the hatch, watching him hose down the concrete slab.

Pointing to the dark blotches on the floor, I say, "You know, those look like police crime marks, the ones that show the outline of the victim."

He looks up from the dark reservoir. "Yeah, well, this is a rat. The mice seem to float."

"Why can't we keep them from getting in?"

"Look at the cistern! We never finished up around the bottom, and the styrofoam is decomposing. The flickers are making holes around the sides, and the roof is lifting. They can get in any old way."

But there's only one way out.

🦌

Years ago our friend Jim Vidocy was staying at the house and couldn't get the water to run. He phoned Jay in late July: "I don't know what to do. I've walked up and down the creek all day. I checked couplings, and opened and closed the valves."

Jay was patient. "There's probably an air lock somewhere in the system."

Jim moaned, "I'm exhausted. I've tried everything. I figure it's a zen koan. The water's in the creek. The water won't come out of the creek."

🐾

Twenty years later the water still won't come out. One week after Jay's departure, the system is dry again. I battle through dogwood leaves, false Solomon seal and elfin capped thimbleberry. From a spiderwebbed cleft in the canyon wall, I squeeze myself up the ledge and back onto the hillside. I could slip over the edge of the cliff, plummet twenty feet into the creek's crevasse, break my leg or hit my head. Nobody would know.

I stagger downhill under the searing sun, through bunchgrass and cheatgrass, following a stitch of pipeline that threads over and under rocks and fallen logs. The land has gone to seed. My boots are pierced with speargrass; they will prick and needle forever. Stumbling onto the flat stretch below, I pick up the pipe. It's hollow and light.

Empty.

🐾

At the Naramata coffee house, I'm having coffee with our old friend Alex. "Did you ever read 'The Coming Anarchy,' by Jonathan Kaplan?" I ask him. "His premise is that resource scarcity, like water or energy, will drive future world conflict."

He laughs. "Do I have to read the book? We're already becoming anarchy." He is referring to the scandal a few years back over a water use permit for a proposed golf course, an issue that splintered the community. Since then a new irrigation system has been installed in Naramata.

Alex is visibly drooping. "You know, that has turned neighbour against neighbour, friend against friend. I've lost some of my oldest friends over this water business..."

❧

The Granite Farm is outside the Naramata Irrigation District. Water from Chute Creek supports this household with cooking and washing water. Without irrigation, the aspen leaves around the house droop like flags unfurled on a windless day. Water adds depth, texture and growth; produces habitat for birds and cottontail rabbits; cools the house; provides shelter from the heat and foils us from blast-from-the-past sunlight. Water supports a flutter of green outside the house — a rowan tree, two saskatoon bushes, scale-ridden aspens, and a tiny peach tree that lays furry eggs of rock-hard fruit.

Without shade, we're cooked.

Juvenile black bear.

🦌 15 🦌
Home Invasions

Nature is not a place to visit, it is home ...

– GARY SNYDER, THE PRACTICE OF THE WILD

I am the homecoming queen! Sometimes it seems that I spend more time coming and going than being here. I wake up in the middle of the night and can't remember where I am. My heart pounds from dragging water and groceries and supplies up the hill in the heat. Walking up to the house with an arthritic hip is slow and painful.

I can't keep this up. Maybe I'm doing penance for youth and hubris. Who do I think I am? Princess Summer-Fall-Winter-Spring? Just what am I trying to prove?

Maybe the dream was just that.

Maybe 'living in beauty' is not enough.

Living here was never easy. Does hanging on to a bad idea make it any better? Why am I still married to this place? Where is Jay when I need him? Why can't he take more time off work to be here with me?

Maybe Thomas Wolfe was right. You can't go home again.

But you can't leave, either!

🦌

6:00 p.m. Vancouver: Time for dinner. I take the bus downtown, meet Jay for a movie or a walk along the beach. Bright lights, big city!

6:00 p.m. Naramata: Time for a quick walk before the sun is down - out the door, down the path, down the hill to the road. Maybe if Margie's home, we can take Rufus for a walk.

But tonight, dust drywalls the place; the knapweed is scratchy, and the sun has sucked the life out of me. I wait until the sun drops into Peachland and the lake is burnished by night and the wind begins to breathe. By then it's too dark. I'm too tired to climb down to the road and back. I worry about bears.

It's 8:00 p.m. The front door gnaws open and shut as if ghosts are drifting in. But it's only the breeze.

Maybe I'm an empty-nester, but the nest isn't empty. The ecology of the house continues to morph, welcoming an array of new tenants: yellow jackets, carpet beetles, black widow spiders, wolf spiders, mice, packrats, box elder bugs, ants...

Ants. Enervated by summer heat, I'm getting ready for bed when a conga line of pulsating ants squirms above the bathroom sink. The wall seethes with tiny scribbles. They're everywhere, scrimshawed lines of tiny, moving creatures. As I swipe at them with toilet paper the parade becomes a nightmare: lines of ants become legions, battalions, a war zone of pulsing, ceaseless lines. I find old ant traps, puncture the holes at the side and set them on the counter. Then I read the small print: 'Traps will be effective within one or two weeks.'

Lysol from under the kitchen counter seems to work. It cleans the walls, and stops ants dead! (Like the music from the Pink Panther, "Dead ant, dead ant, deadant, deadant, deadant....") Soon the sponge is caked with ants - ants in the tiny holes, ants lining the sides. They scurry up my arms and legs. Ants in my pants!

The next morning I am making tea when I first see them. Streams of ants cross the kitchen counter, run up the curtains, then down into the tea and spice cupboard. Armed with Lysol, I wipe them off with paper towel, which is soon peppered by ant carcasses, squirming ants, acrobatic ants doing backbends and downward facing dog. Ants fall onto my arms and my legs in a script of movement. They're coming from nowhere!

Just a minute! The honey jar, at the back of the cupboard, is fuzzy with life. Strings of hairy ants run up and down the sides. Omigod! Inside the jar they seethe and fuzz like an animated cartoon, bebopping and crazy with movement. I jerk the honey jar into the sink and the lid flies off. Good God! The inside pulses with ants. An ecstasy of ants. Ants, ants, ants. Try a soupçon of this, Peter Mayle!

❦

I try gardening, a variation on the 100-metre diet, to provide food for the eyes and habitat for birds. Next time I'm in Penticton, I'm poking through the plants at Art Knapp's, ogling springtime red geraniums, purple pink frills of pelargoniums and happy yellow pansies, all bursting with desire and genetic engineering, clamouring to reproduce.

"Do you have flowering plants that are drought resistant?" I ask.

Michelle, a sturdy woman with a wild spikey hairdo and a British accent marches me to the other side of the lot, where nothing is in bloom. She reminds me of my no-nonsense 8th grade gym teacher.

"This is our xeriscape section," she says tersely, pointing to a small array of cinquefoil, mock orange, and saskatoon.

But I'm into nonsense. "Do you have anything else, like a deciduous tree that doesn't need much water?"

"No." Michelle nods her head back and forth definitively. *These people! They just don't get it. What does she want, ever-blooming, low maintenance, grows well on rock?*

She says, slowly, as if I'm a 12-year-old, "There are Russian olives next to the highway by Redwing Resorts. They're hardy."

Then she turns abruptly to the couple behind me, whose cart is crammed with decorative grass and tortured rose spikes. She chirps, " And how can I help you?"

I always hated gym class. Except for dancing.

❦

I have learned to survive up here by myself. But I worry about:

- fire;
- break-ins;
- bears;
- mice and rats;
- lugging everything up and down to the house
- falling or hurting myself and having nobody find me.

It doesn't work. I can't innoculate myself by expecting the worst. Am I just too soft? Lazy? Is it based on fear? Maybe I've just gotten stuck. Over thirty years of stuck. I try to accept suffering and impermanence.

This is some kind of Zen, all right!

Does the spell of landscape last forever? Does E.O. Williams's 'biophilia,' the attraction to place, only apply to the place where you are raised? For all who are migrants, newcomers, or immigrants, how do we craft our sense of place? Just living here has become my craft. I work on the path, talk to my neighbours and observe wildlife.

But this is not enough to conserve this landscape. The personal does not directly fuse the political. My musings do not deflect the forces of development changing this valley.

❦

In early September, when I open the living-room blinds, my eyes catch a silvery hue. I'm seeing something that doesn't fit, that looks like marsh cinquefoil, the potentilla I've seen in the Squamish Estuary in Howe Sound, above muddy flats where waves lap at seagrass and alder thickets - about as different an environment from the dry Okanagan as I can fathom.

I step out on the side porch to check. The rowan tree, the one that Eleanor gave us when Phoebe was born almost 30 years ago, is shattered! Its branches are broken and torn, leaves dusty and limp. Most of the branches are snapped off, and all the berries, except for four hard-as-rock timbits, have been stripped clean.

"Damned bears!!" I yell out to nobody in particular. "Assholes! You shithead bears." I'm really frightened. "Idiot bears!! Stupid bloody bears!!!"

When I venture out front to look around, I find piles of bear shit under the front porch. The bear has even pooped on the front porch next to the picnic table. I've never had to deal with a bear in residence! A bear that has already staked a claim!

The next day a California quail plumps down for a dust bath in the trail, and then scoots off under the juniper, his cocky plume perched just above his head. A redbreasted nuthatch scuttles at the feeder, while pine siskins pester the pine tree.

Oh, hello! It's getting dark at 7:30 when a black roly-poly bear tumbles up onto the top of the rim. She galumphs across the front of the house, making her way for the fallen rowan tree. Aha! The perp returns to the scene of the crime. I grab two pot lids and dash out on the porch yelling, "GO! GO! Get out of here you bloody bear!"

The clang of lids is a methamphetamined temple call - speedy, metallic and loud. The bear tucks back on her hind legs as I yell and clang the pot lids. Snapping and snuffing, she challenges this affront to her turf. Not good. A bear with attitude. A furry, half-grown bundle of bear that could have a mother in the vicinity.

I start to carry pot lids with me, even just to go to the car. Like an L.A. cop, I'm "packin!" Not heat, but sound! I sing, and shout, and it sounds like the Salvation Army is camped next door. The next night, when I walk out in front of the house, the bear is climbing up over the rim. This time she scampers away when she sees me. I buy an air horn - a bear horn – at Canadian Tire, and practice until my hearing is gone.

                ❧

I try comfort foods.

I'm back at the house with a rhubarb plant and a raspberry bush. I bought the raspberry at Art Knapp's. The rhubarb, from Walmart, is a disaster. The bag, when I unpack it from its box, is tropical with condensation; its long pink tendrils pulse into heat and light in a murky Swan Lake, squirming back and forth until they're strangled in their tight plastic bag, all mud and root and long ruby squid-like shoots, each flopping a small anemic green leaf at the end.

Neither survive the summer.

                ❧

This fall term I've been granted leave from teaching to revise a book on environmental policy. In the first week of October, scarlet, flame-thrower branches of sumac are ready to drop, not just one leaf at a time; the entire compound stalk of leaves fades all at once. Outside the window, aspen leaves spatter the ground, butterscotch and gold. There is solace in the dregs of summer, the first breath of autumn and winter.

After a day of drizzle, Brent Mountain is illuminated by snow. Kinglets, juncos, chickadees and one pesky Steller's jay bustle about the feeder.

Night comes early. By 8 p.m. a necklace of light rings the lakeshore, but the new moon hides in an inkjet sky, and the stars forget to shine.

A ravine of darkness surrounds the house.

The next night Okanagan Lake spreads beneath a perfect sunset of clamshell pinks and blue-grey clouds. The tap drips, the fridge hums, and I swoon to a symphony of soft sounds. I am a long way from neighbours or any other light. I exhale and stars sprinkle the heavens.

Suddenly, branches and logs clatter from the wood pile on the front porch. I jump to my feet and run to turn on the porch light. I see nothing. I sit back down in my favorite chair, waiting, with the light still on. Soon there is another skatter of sound, as if some poltergeist were rearranging the firewood. Then silence.

For the next hour, a frantic but erratic force scuttles around the house. The sounds are sudden and unpredictable. Tiny feet skedaddle. Then nothing. Gnawing, nudging sounds, a crash and more scampering of feet. When I look outside, on the porch, I don't see a thing.

> Wood rats are of no agricultural significance because of
> their rocky habitat and foliage diet. Their attraction to
> deserted buildings, however, makes them a nuisance of some
> economic importance. Given sufficient time they can wreck
> the interior of a cabin and render it almost uninhabitable.

– BANFIELD, MAMMALS OF CANADA

I phone Jay for advice and consolation. While I'm talking on the phone, a tiny nose and whiskers, the paws, and finally an entire grey body and puffy packrat tail parade back and forth on the window sill on the front porch, just two feet away on the other side of the glass, sniffing for a way to get in.

I drop the phone and lurch across the room, open the front door, and scream at the rat, sweeping the broom in a frenzy of motion. I slam and lock the door (because they are such canny creatures) and return to the phone.

"You'd better set the trap," Jay advises.

I bait the Hav-a-Hart with peanut butter on a cracker, and place it on the side porch. Once in bed, I jam in my earplugs, read about Tuscany, and listen for the metallic clunk of the trap. During the night I hear the rat clinking around the cage. The next morning, enclosed in the grillwork, the soft grey fur, whiskers, beady little black eyes, and long furry tail of a packrat await liberation.

Above the KVR tracks, I open the trap under a clump of pines. Petit raton sniffs cautiously at the open door policy, then scuttles into the pine needle duff. But relocation doesn't work for bears! What is its success rate with rats? I could paint fingernail polish on rodent digits to identify them. And I could seek funding under the Attorney-General's office, a grant for the rehabilitation of rodent offenders, an attempt to mitigate woodrat recidivism.

Back at the house, I attack the porch, as if cleanliness and order were rodent prophylactics. The old apple box used to store kindling is lined with rat shit and cactus spines. I should be wearing a respirator. Holding my breath against Hanta Virus, I start to clean up. I sweep the porch, restack the firewood, and settle down. The sun sets, the fridge purrs, the wind whistles outside.

I am reading in bed, waiting for the new moon to oreo the night. Suddenly baby Thumper drumrolls in the attic just above my head.

Oh no! Does this happen in Provence?

We could lose our three-star rating!

❧

The next morning, I gaze out my back window at the lake elbowing north under Okanagan Mountain. Today my e-mail includes an "Ecocritical" Call for Papers:

CRITICAL ECOLOGIES: EPISTEMOLOGIES OF NATURE:
KNOWING AND WRITING THE NATURAL WORLD

New School of Social Research, New York City, 12-15 July, 2010.

While the legacy of classical humanism is imbued with a culture/nature dualism, more recent developments in ecocritism investigate the range of human relationships with the natural world. This conference explores the integration of the self and the natural world through the development of an ecocritical dialogue.

This conference will interrogate the notion of 'nature' in the built environment. Participants are invited to explore the relations between ecology and culture within the 'natural' labora-tory of New York City, which includes such diverse simulacra as the Museum of Natural History and the Bronx Zoo.

Possible presentations might include:

- *Rural depopulation and the urbanization of ecology*
- *Beyond Wilderness: Post-colonial, post-urban, post-wild?*
- *Taxonomies as Natural World Order(ing)*
- *The Electronic Call of the Wild: Skitter, Bogs, and ZooTube*
- *Science / Fiction: Nature Writing that Sells!*
- *Pack Rats as "Other": Reconciling the Scurry Furry*

Deadline for submissions: December 18, 2009
Contact: Professor Anhinga von Rappoport (avrapport@nssr.com)

❧

The next time I'm at the house, a gnawing sound scrapes from the attic. It seems to be coming from just above the Clivus toilet vent, maybe on the roof. A packrat is trying to get into the attic, and then it is only a matter of time before it will eat its way into the main floor of the house. It's happened before.

The wobbly aluminum ladder clatters as I set it up beneath the hatch, armed with my tools: flashlight, workgloves, steel wool. Beneath the attic's geometry of trusses floats an ocean of billowing pink fiberglass insulation, peppered with old mouse and rat droppings. I pull myself up, grabbing the rafters and stepping only on the edge of the trusses, to avoid springing the traps (the Have-No-Heart kind) or stepping on the ceiling (because I'd go right through). I swing my way like Curious George over to the fan. It's hopeless: I can't deconstruct my way out of here. I'm at the Granite Farm to be "in nature", but only with preferred species. The ceiling of the house is pinpricked with light, where shingles are loose or the house has shifted. These are all possible entries for mice. Yuck!

After stuffing more steel wool around the vent stack, I monkeyswing back to the trapdoor. One deer mouse is dead in a sprung trap. I hold the trap between my thumb and index finger and take it down the ladder. Outside the house, I cross the crusty rock plateau, then lift the spring to roll the body into a small crevice. Wee mousie is a soft, supple taupe grey; its tail hangs limply and its whiskers catch the sun - clear, like tiny bites of fishing line. Nestled in the rock, its tiny toes articulate like those of a newborn baby.

This is a problem for the lover of nature. After thirty-five years, my opposition to capital punishment has become theoretical.

The next day I am in line at Walmart, buying a rat trap when the woman behind me leans over and says, "Too bad my dad's not around any longer." I raise my eyebrows. What does she mean?

"He'd come out and shoot 'em for you."

❦ 16 ❦
Under Fire

September 6, 1914. Not a drop of rain has fallen since August 16th ... Everything is parched ... Forest fires are raging in all parts of the country. The air is thick with a blue haze of smoke which occasionally thickens to brown clouds from which fall little flakes of white ash. The days are no longer so very hot, & the nights are quite chilly.

**— JOHN SUGARS, AN OKANAGAN HISTORY: THE DIARIES OF
ROGER JOHN SUGARS, 1905-1919**

August 23, 2003

In Vancouver, there is a phone message from our Naramata neighbours: "Hi Jay. This is Margie. They've told us we have to evacuate. The fire's coming down pretty fast. Last we heard it was at Squally Point. It's pretty smoky up here. We're going to be up at Apex in the camper."

Jay's already on the road when I wake up the next morning; his bike is gone too. I call him on his cell phone.

"I'm just clearing Chilliwack. I want to be up there in case anything changes."

"O.K. But don't try to go out to the house. There's nothing you can do."
He's abrupt. "Don't worry. I'll stay with Robbie in town, or in a motel."
Sure.

❦

Jay tells the story like this:

Coming downhill on the Coquihalla, the smoke is so thick that I can't see a thing. As
I drive past Peachland, I pull over and look across the lake, but all I can see is tiny flares of
flame. It's like I'm looking into a fog. When I get to Penticton I head straight to Canadian
Tire and buy a headlamp and a bunch of hose end fittings — sprinklers and nozzles.. Then I
head north out the Naramata Road. At Bancroft's there's a road block with a Mountie.

'I've got a place up there," I say, "with a gate on it."

The guy doesn't say anything. I try again. "I've got a key to open the gate."

The guy looks grim. 'We don't need your key, we've got bulldozers.'

"Well, there are easier ways to open the gate than with a bulldozer."

'We'll see about that.'

❦

I don't put up any fuss. I just turn around, drive back towards town, and start up
Smethurst. But the RCMP has a roadblock on the KVR too, so I turn back down. It's too
obvious to leave the car up here, so I park down at the Naramata Centre.

Then I throw my stuff into the pack, and ride the bike back up Smethurst. Just below
the line of sight of the barricade, I zip up a driveway, lift my bike over a fence, and carry it
uphill, through boulders and riprap from the railway, so nobody will see me. The smoke is
thick. You can smell and taste it. I'm operating on adrenalin, sweaty and out of breath by the
time I get on the railroad track.

Mel calls me on my cell: "Jay, where the hell are you? What's happening?"

"I'm almost at the tunnel. It looks like the end of the earth. Everything's dark, and it's
just after noon. Look, I'll call you back later. There's a car up here."

Two young kids in a big old boat of a car are trawling the tracks. One of them says, "You know, there's a fire up here."

"Yeah, looks like it." I'm cool.

They look at one another, and back at me. "What are you doing up here?"

"Oh, I'm just getting some exercise."

They turn the car around and head down. "You better watch it," they yell from the car. "That fire's getting close."

❧

I get to Glenfir but I hear somebody driving up the Chute Lake road, so I throw the bike under the trees, and scoot down in the pine needle duff as a big truck thunders past. Then I ride down through Watson's to our place. It sounds like a war zone up towards Chute Lake, with the drone of water bombers and the thwack of helicopter blades. The fire roars like a jet engine.

When I get to the house, I pick up some tools and patch up the water line where they cut it at the road. Then I go up to the creek to start it back up. I try to get the sprinklers going up on the roof, but there isn't enough pressure, so I bring them down and put them around the house. Thank God the wind has gone around to the south. If it had stayed from the north, the house would be gone and the fire would be in downtown Naramata by now.

Last night the fire came all the way down from Squally Point, splitting east to Chute Lake and south down Okanagan Lake. It's coming down the mountain as if it's rushing up an elevator shaft, with flames spurting thousands of feet in the air. A mushroom-shaped cloud towers to about 30,000 feet, like there's been a nuclear attack!

I pick up things to take with me and put them in the backpack next to the door - Keltie's quilt, photos from Mom and Phoebe's pictures. The bike's all set to go. If the fire comes over the ridge I'll whip down our hill and out the main road. If worse comes to worse, I can climb down the creek to the lake and grab whatever boat is handy.

❧

We're supposed to have been evacuated, so I keep the shades drawn so it looks like nobody's home. I tune the little portable TV set to Kelowna. Here I sit, in a dark house that reeks of smoke, watching TV to see what's happening outside. I'm eating canned soup out of the cupboard. I use my headlamp. It feels like the power to the house has been cut off.

From time to time, I climb up the bluff behind the house. Above the ridge, it looks like the Lake Louise campground, with flares and flickers from hundreds of fires all the way up into Okanagan Mountain Park. I watch a helicopter lay down a strip of burning fire, like napalm, to burn uphill. The backburn collides with the burn coming down from Chute Lake. The road I biked down earlier is in flames.

I keep climbing up and down the back ridge, watching them fight the fire, making sure it's not going to come in this direction. It's like I'm in a balcony in a theatre, almost on top of the crews. The wind has gone around now and it's cleared up so I can see. Guys are moving around with skidders, pulling tanks, spraying whenever they find a hot spot. They're cutting trees with chainsaws to create gaps so that the fire can't jump. I feel like I should be down there helping these guys, but there's still too much to do at the house.

By one a.m. I'm done in. I crash for fifteen or twenty minutes or so, and then one eye pops open, and I check to make sure flames aren't coming over the ridge. To the north, the sky glows orange. If I smell new smoke, I'm going to have to move fast. I'm ready to leave at a moment's notice.

The next day, the wind has gone flat. Water bombers and helicopters with hurricane buckets circle over the lake, and then back above Harrises, hitting the fire again and again. Meanwhile, I rake and cart needles and duff from the big pine in front of the porch out to the logging road. Twenty-five loads from just one tree! In between, I climb back up on top on the ridge and watch.

Back in the city, the phone rings and I know it's Jay.

"Good morning, Vietnam." He's doing his rendition of the Robin Williams movie, as helicopters thwackwhackwhackwhackwhack overhead.

"What saved us so far is that the wind has gone around to the south, and there is no more combustible material. And these guys! They've been working flat out."

I'm still worried. "Just make sure you can get out! Stop trying to be so heroic."

"You know I can't leave the house. Besides, the bike's ready. Downhill to the lake, and then I'll take Kate's kayak out, or borrow somebody else's boat. I'm all set."

I ask myself, what is it with this guy?

❦

That night at the Granite Farm, the wind picks up from the south. I'm still glued to the television, watching the fire as it moves north to Kelowna. Hey wait, isn't that Tony Conlon, who lives up the hill? He says that they had to fight tooth and nail to protect the houses at Glenfir. And this one!

Right now the fire is hip-hopping its way into Kelowna, right over the break, like it's not even there. I climb up and down the ridge dozens of times, to make sure there aren't any flare-ups. There aren't as many guys here now; they must have moved some of them to Kelowna.

The third day, the wind slows down; it feels like it's coming from the north again. It socks back in, and the place is so smoky I can't see the lake. It's hard to tell if the fire is going again. Debris is falling out of the air, but nothing is smoldering or lit up. I'm still on edge.

❦

On the fourth day, I ride my bike back out the way I came. I've got to get back to work. They're still mopping up. I wheel my bike up Watson's road. When a truck comes along I sneak back into the woods. The uphill side of the road is scorched. I ride back down the KVR to Smethurst. The RCMP is at the barricade.

"Where have you been?" She's Quebecoise. "Don't you know that this area is closed?"

I can't tell her where I've been, or why I've been out there. I can't tell her that thirty years of my life almost went up in smoke. That I could never get it back.

"I've just been getting some exercise, you know, riding on the KVR."

"You weren't supposed to be up there! There is a fire!"

"I know about that. I could see a lot of smoke up there."*What if she opens my packsack, with all the artwork and photos? She'll think I've been looting the place!*

I peddle down to the car. By Merritt, the smoke starts to dissipate. The whole province needs a respirator.

❦

By August 28, 2003, the evacuation has been lifted! I talk to Margie, my neighbour, on the phone. She says: "It's smoky, but it's great to be back. They saved your place, but it was close. The fire burned uphill from the ranch, right to your property line."

The Okanagan Mountain Park Fire has been front page news for almost a week. People and places I know have become The News at Six. And Nine. And Ten. Every hour, even on the half hour. After the fire turned north from our place, it burned hundreds of houses in Kelowna. It's still burning.

Jay was there, but I need to see it for myself. How close did the fire come? What about the big ponderosa? Is the house still in danger?

As I drive north on the Naramata Road the smoke-washed sky is dull, the air flat, the lake deadpan grey. There are no other cars and no tractors; the landscape is lifeless, deflated. I scan north to Squally Point but the faded ridge of Okanagan Mountain descends to the lake like it always does. Except for the hazy light, nothing seems to have changed.

There are signs. On people's lawns, tacked on trees: "FIREFIGHTERS, THANKS!", "We owe you, Firefighters!" and just plain "Thanks!'

As I drive over the cattleguard, several trucks lumber down the road towards me - pick-ups and a water tanker. Local fire departments, forestry crews and reserve units are en route to Kelowna, where the fire blazes on.

At the roadblock, the RCMP officer leans towards me, a young guy with a face like an old man's, sober and gaunt. "Remember, you're still on evacuation alert. You must be prepared to vacate in an hour's notice."

Now that I'm here, I'm afraid to go up to the house. It's like the scene of an accident. I need to see the place, but I don't want to look.

I stop in to see Margie, and we dance into one another's arms as if we're in a V-day movie. She waves me into the kitchen, recounting her story of the evacuation. "You couldn't see what was happening because of the smoke, even from across the lake. When it lifted, people kept calling me on my cell phone to say the house was still here."

Margie is a frontier woman – smart, no-nonsense and self-reliant. She can fix anything, and has an opinion on everything. Sometimes you have to work to get it out of her, but not today! She has spent days watching and waiting, steeling herself to kiss it all goodbye.

"I finally figured out that I could just call home to see if it was still there. If the answering machine picked up, then I knew the house was still standing."

We sit at the kitchen table, peering uphill. From here, nothing seems to have changed. The place is foggy with smoke, but the main characters – road, cliffs, mountains and the lake – are all in their usual place. There is still a sense of foreboding, that it could happen again. Maybe you could call it "postboding."

Across the road at Paradise Ranch, soft bushy ponderosa branches cushion the air, but their rusty-hued needles look like the sepia wash of an old photo album. It's as if the fire burned hundreds of years ago, not last week.

Margie's golden retriever Rufus suddenly jumps to his feet and pads over to the kitchen door, nails clicking on the tiles, and tail wagging. A few seconds later, Sandy, whose place tucks in beneath Margie's, waltzes in.

"I've got this big rattler under my porch, and I can't get rid of it. What'll I do?" We all laugh. This is normal. Rattlers, leaky irrigation pipes, car trouble - a return to everyday life!

Margie offers us a beer, even though it's just mid-afternoon, and I listen to the girls' version of the fire. Sandy, the drama queen, vamps around the kitchen:

"Once you left, you couldn't get back out here. So I used the lipstick and Tim Horton's approach. Told them I just wanted to come back out and get a few things I'd left behind. I left a box of donuts with the guys at the gate. It worked! I wanted to see how Gray was doing. You know, he said he'd never leave his place. And he had the horses to take care of, too. Swore he'd stay 'til the end."

"Yeah," chimes in Margie. "It's a guy thing. They insisted they'd stick it out, you know, defend the turf. Gray stayed, and Danny was up there, and Tony, up at Glenfir, and Jay. But the women were smarter, and most of the guys, too. There was really nothing anybody could do. When that wind comes up, it's terrifying. We had to go."

Sandy pipes in. "The hard thing was, what to take? What's my absolute favorite thing? What do I need for the rest of my life? Pictures of my mom and dad, the kids' stuff, artwork? How can you pack a lifetime's memories into one car? Everything means something."

🕯

I open the gate and drive up the two-track road, past thick sprays of antelope brush, grey-green sage, golden wands of bunchgrass. All of this is fuel. The sere landscape looks sunburned like any late summer day, but thickened by autumn haze.

I pant up the path to the house, struggling with duffle bags. I try not to inhale too much smoke, but I'm gasping in minutes. The fine-toothed parchment of saskatoon rattles against my bags. A dark confetti of blackened aspen leaves and charbroiled ponderosa bark spatters the trail. Except for my ragged breathing, everything is still.

At the top, I stagger towards the log house, which fades into the smoke-stained light like the relic of an old mining camp. The cabin is bleached by thirty years of heat and sunlight, its shake roof tufted by flits of moss, the front porch so dry it splinters just from my gaze. I am home.

But "home" is a stack of kindling: logs, firewood, unused lumber, books, newspapers. The house reeks of burnt toast. I walk from room to room, savouring pictures, my rocking chair and the curtains I sewed by hand. To the north, the rocky outcrop in back of the house shuts off the view of the fire's remains. Looking south, the view to Penticton is blurred, as if I'm looking through a smeared camera lens.

It's like a nightmare. Maybe nothing happened. Maybe I'll wake up and everything will be the way it was.

The next day, I sneak from the back of my place uphill in the direction of Okanagan Park. Stands of airhead ponderosas have been vaporized. Under foot, ash-covered soil traces game trails and fallen logs. Hillsides are firewashed to bedrock. Black skeletal pines spike the Death Valley sky. Shadow trees with grey-green needles and blackened bark are the living dead.

The scorched earth policy is alleviated here and there by patches of olive-green pines. Life may come back to the forest. But not in my lifetime.

For now it's painted black. A still life.

🦌

The fire reveals our house as a textbook case of what not to do. How could sparse rock outcrops dotted with microbiotic soil and bunchgrass burn so intensely, with such speed? Xeriscaped landscaping may save water and maintain natural habitat, but it is no firewall. And we've left pines and juniper near the house for shade and bird cover. The fire reveals this place as nothing but fuel, inside and out - furniture and logs, juniper, antelope brush and yellow pine.

Building a house here, we changed this place. It is no longer 'natural', but something we need to protect. If not for wind, firemen and luck, the house would have been incinerated, integrated seamlessly into the environment.

We may have been thinking 'outside the box' to build the house here.

But we weren't thinking beyond the box.

Up in a log house on a rocky bluff overlooking Okanagan Lake, Tina Turner prances around the living room, belting out a Bonnie Raitt blues. She darts over to the piano and picks out the notes to a song, then gets up and belts it out over a proscenium of sagebrush, rabbitbrush and saskatoon. Who does she think she is, Snow White, with a chipmunk audience at the windows? Is this the wild-side karaoke bar?

(It's in A minor if you want to hum along.)

TORCH SONG

> Well, it's another dry spell, and only time will tell
> As I look out on the cracklin' leaves.
> I chase away my fear by wishing you were here
> But somewhere there's a fire, burning
> Somewhere there's a fire that burns ...

It started late one night with a lightning strike,
Somewhere in the hills north of town;
Then in just two days the whole mountain was ablaze
And the fire ... came a rumbling down.

The phone started ringing, then a knock at my door,
And I knew it was time to go.
I couldn't find my keys or leave my memories,
So I just thought I'd better lie low.

Chorus:
It sounded just like a train, and it moved faster than a plane
Woo, ooo, ooo, aaaaahhhh
Then the sky turned to night with the darkening light
Of the smoke, and the afterglow.

The clouds piled up higher in a crimson glow
And I didn't know which way to turn,
Because the smoke filled the valley and my lungs and my head
And the fire just had to burn.

Then I looked outside, saw you waitin' with my ride,
A firefighter tired and worn.
You've said 'we've gotta get clear, you can't stay here
If you want to see another morn.

So I shut the door on the life that I knew.
You guided me down through the maze
Of wind, and smoke and pine. We passed the fire line.
We'd finally outrun the blaze.

Chorus:
It sounded just like a train, and it moved faster than a plane
Woo, ooo, ooo, aaaaahhhh
Then the sky turned to night with the darkening light
Of the smoke, and the afterglow.

I've never forgotten how you looked at me then
Though you never got to tell me your name
My whole world just vanished right up in smoke
And things will never be the same -
No things will never be the same.

The melody needs some work.

♥

It's six weeks since the fire when Jay and I stop at the intersection of the Chute Lake Road to talk with the woman staffing the tent-trailer. The road up to the lake is still closed. "It's Day 40 for me." she says. "I've been here since August 23rd."

When we drive past the turnoff two days later, the barricade is down and the trailer is gone. There are no signs that anything has happened, but in the distance the ridgeline of Okanagan Mountain Park rises in a high, blackened swath.

Uphill from our place, things are already beginning to change. The acrid, burnt smell has lifted and plants are starting to grow - clover-like clusters of knapweed and the sawtooth trim of wild rose leaves. Sprouts of saskatoon announce an unseasonal spring. New oregon grape prickles like holly from the cracked soil.

There are signs of other life as well. Bear tracks, mother and cub, pad through silty soil. On one of our walks, a young deer, probably some motherless child, jerks towards us tentatively like a marionette on a string, then springs away.

I'm beginning to accept this pardon, to live with some degree of grace. There will never be closure. Last night it rained, hard, like a thousand mice scrambling over the roof. Just in time for Thanksgiving.

❦ 17 ❦
Ecological Niche

The South Okanagan and Lower Similkameen has long been recognized as a region that combines a tremendous diversity of habitats with unique species, many of which are found nowhere else in the province or in Canada ... it is now one of the four most endangered ecosystems in our country.

– GOVERNMENT OF BRITISH COLUMBIA, MINISTRY OF ENVIRONMENT, HABITAT ATLAS FOR WILDLIFE AT RISK, SOUTH OKANAGAN AND LOWER SIMILKAMEEN

Two white-tailed deer hurtle over the cliff and spring across the rock in front of the house, leaping out of my field of vision in a jerky ballet. Sproing! I dash out to the front porch to watch them, as a smaller, quicker movement darts onto the scene. Dogs! Two of our neighbour Matt's dogs are on the scent, running the deer, yapping and already out of sight.

When we arrived, roads and creek marked property lines; most of the boundaries of this place were transparent. The creation of Okanagan Mountain Park in 1973 meant open space north to Kelowna. No fences tatooed the horizon; you could walk almost anywhere. But over the decades, natural areas have been closing in, as humans, houses, dogs, cats, guns, ATV's and skidoos encroach on wild spaces. By 2009, it's all one big off-leash area.

Out in our neck of the grasslands, newcomers mix in with the old. Margie and Tom have built a new house downhill, Alex has moved into Naramata, and many of the houses at Indian Rock below us have changed hands. Above the Naramata townsite, new subdivisions stretch out above the railway. This spring as the car scrambles uphill, the creek is barely audible against the low roar of four-laned Highway #97 across the lake. As the valley succumbs to development, is it possible to maintain its ecological integrity?

This piece of land rims the northern edge of the South Okanagan landscape. Among the four dominant ecological classifications of this region – riparian, forest, grassland and rugged terrain – the latter is our most appropriate signature. The Granite Farm contains one of the northernmost stands of antelope-brush in North America, linking British Columbia to the Columbia Basin of the Pacific Northwest, a dry, open topography of sparse badlands and deserts.

The antelope-brush ecosystem is ... home to 88 species considered at risk ... In the South Okanagan, 60 percent of its historic range has vanished ... Urbanization has been responsible for the loss of about 16 percent of antelope-brush habitat, the other 84 percent to agriculture – vineyards, cultivated fields, orchards and grazed pasture ... if the current rates of loss continue, all antelope-brush will be gone by 2026 outside of protected areas and steep slopes ...

– LARRY PYNN, THE VANCOUVER SUN, OCTOBER 20, 2003

There is no Office of Homeland Security for those threatened species that call the South Okanagan home. Our property too is becoming an endangered space, an "island" less capable of supporting indigenous species with the development of its surrounds. Our own improvements further fragment this habitat – one more access road means one less badger. I lie on the old rumpled sofa reading the travel section of the Vancouver Sun. Why is the exotic - Tuscany or Provence - always somewhere else?

SOUTH OKANAGAN-LOWER SIMILKAMEEN SPECIES AT RISK

REPTILES and AMPHIBIANS: Tiger Salamander, Great Basin Spadefoot Toad, Painted Turtle, Rubber Boa, Racer, Gopher Snake, Night Snake, Western Rattlesnake
BIRDS: American Bittern, Great Blue Heron, Sandhill Crane, Long-billed Curlew, Prairie Falcon, Flammulated Owl, Western Screech Owl, Short-eared Owl, Lewis's Woodpecker, White-headed Woodpecker, Canyon Wren, Sage Thrasher, Yellow-breasted Chat, Brewer's Sparrow, Lark Sparrow, Grasshopper Sparrow, Bobolink;
MAMMALS: Fringed Myotis, Western Red Bat, Spotted Bat, Townsend's Big-eared Bat, Pallid Bat, Badger, California Bighorn Sheep

– GOVERNMENT OF BRITISH COLUMBIA, MINISTRY OF ENVIRONMENT. HABITAT ATLAS FOR WILDLIFE AT RISK, SOUTH OKANAGAN LOWER SIMILKAMEEN

As rush hour traffic simmers in Penticton, coyote pads down the Granite Farm road in the early morning. Its single-file footprints track the frosting of silt that sifts downhill. Coyote stops to sniff where a snake track scrolls across the puffy road like an exercise in cursive writing. It pads

off the track where the three-pronged prints of quail arrow the dust. Coyote filters downhill, golden eyes gilded by early morning sun, brindled body blending into the leftover straw of yarrow and bunchgrass.

A black-tipped osprey circles its nest in a Douglas fir, clutching a fish from the fast-food outlet where the creek meets Okanagan Lake. I think about how this new road makes its small contribution, fragmenting habitat, compacting soil, and introducing weeds. It meanders through fountains of antelope-brush that fan uphill from the gate. Their straggly branches arch over sparse terrain, spiced in cinnamon blooms that attract bees and butterflies. The hillside vibrates with motion and sound.

A mule deer munches bottle-brush branches of antelope-brush, chomping toothed wedge-shaped leaves like a weed-eater. The radar headset of mule deer ears drifts slowly down the draw.

Later, as I drive downhill towards town, my tire treads erase the morning.

About 190 species of birds breed in the South Okanagan. Not only is this almost half the Canadian total, but it is probably the highest total for any area of similar size in Canada, and close to the highest in the United States and Canada.

– B.C. GOVERNMENT, MINISTRY OF ENVIRONMENT, HABITAT ATLAS FOR WILDLIFE AT RISK;

I dash up to the Granite Farm in late spring after another year of teaching. Some of my new friends are feathered.

9:00 a.m. Cherry Lane Parking Lot. Birders coo and chirp to one another, laden with backpacks and birdbooks and scopes.

9:10 a.m. Past the big osprey nest, we zoom onto the Channel Parkway to head south to Okanagan Falls and Oliver. We wing past Vaseux Lake

(Coots! Mallards! Widgeons!) and orchards and vineyards (Eastern Kingbirds! Magpie!).

10:15 a.m. From the Husky station in Osoyoos, we carpool uphill to Spotted Lake. Trucks tornado past us, but in their tailspin you can hear birdtalk:

"Kestrel!"

"Violet-greens"

"No, Tree swallows."

"There are both."

"Eagle!," I shout, excited to be the first to spot it.

Someone corrects me. "Turkey vulture." Oh no! How could I have missed the dihedral flight, the two-toned underwing, the soaring pattern?

❦

Birding a century ago was more lucrative:

SEPTEMBER 22, 1911.

The Big horned owl (Bubo Virginianus) is a very fine bird. It measures about 3 feet from tip to tip of the wings. It has beautiful soft down feathers, of a greyish-brown colour. I suppose it is a nocturnal bird, but I have seen quite a lot, in the daytime ... There is a $2.00 bounty on this bird also
$3.00 on Golden Eagles (which are scarce) and $3.00 on Coyotes.

– JOHN SUGARS. AN OKANAGAN HISTORY: THE DIARIES OF ROGER JOHN SUGARS, 1905-1919

A bird in the hand is worth two in the bush!

❦

The Okanagan Similkameen Conservation Alliance hosts a yearly event to celebrate the biodiversity of the South Okanagan. On the Victoria Day weekend, the Meadowlark Festival boasts a cast of thousands: birds, geologists, bats, butterflies, deserts, mountain hikes, bike rides, forest walks, sagebrush strolls, astronomy, owls and raptors, First Nations walks, music, readings, Big Day birding, little days of birding and botany, banquets, lunches, spectators, and speakers. The whole parade! Nature surges through the valley with sunshine and new green growth; migrant species and residents, indigenous and introduced, blooming and breeding and carrying on. Events of choice might include:

Event 93: Hang-Gliding with Raptors. 9:00 to 3:00. Airborne participants will soar with bald and golden eagles, ospreys, turkey vultures, red-tailed hawks, kestrels and other raptors of the South Okanagan. Eye to eye contact with birds of prey! Birds' eye view of the Valley! Learn to see and think like a raptor. Pay and prey! Meet at the parking lot, north end of Skaha Lake. Participants must be in excellent physical condition and willing to sign liability release forms. Charge: $75.

Or maybe this:

Event 457: Bungee-Jumping McIntyre Bluffs. Each journey includes a rapid and intense discovery of ecological transition from mixed coniferous forests to desert terrain. You will glimpse a blurred array of wildflowers, packrat nests and geological history in successive descents (and ascents) from the top of McIntyre Bluff to the valley bottom. Meet at the Habitat Garden of Okanagan College to carpool. Sponsored by Penticton Regional Hospital Emergency Department.

❦

Back above Osoyoos, binoculars and telescopes peer through sagebrush and along roadside fences, like a CSIS surveillance in the bush. "Red-tailed hawk!"

"Bluebirds!" shouts somebody up the road.

"Western?" asks John.

"Look like Mountain from here," says Debbie, collapsing her scope and heading across the road.

It's like Bingo Night in Canada. Jim S. codes the sightings in his notebook. . "Green-winged teal. Over on that far side."

"Oh, yeah, I've got 'em... Is that a Ruddy Duck?"

"Could be. Oh, and look! On the far side. Phalarope!"

Above Osoyoos, our lunch break at Blue Lake features lazuli buntings and western tanagers. Later, as we drive downhill from Kilpoola Lake, the gurgle of sandhill cranes drifts down the Valley.

People in the city ask me, "What do you do all day?"

I guess they've never lived in the country.

❦ 18 ❦
Wine Country

From his back porch, Bryan Hardman can look up to the Naramata Bench... considered some of the best fruit-growing terrain in the country. "This past season, looking along this Bench, it looked like dinosaurs feeding on the trees...With the big excavators just pulling out trees, like boom, boom, boom. At any one spot on the hillside there, you could see six to eight excavators at once, pulling out apple trees.

— WENDY STUECK, GLOBE AND MAIL, OCTOBER 7, 2006. B4

We're driving south on Highway #97, coming from Vancouver. "Hey, did you see that sign saying "Welcome to Wine Country?" I ask. Jay is busy scanning fire damage on Okanagan Mountain across the lake.

I continue, "Who names it, anyway? Did they hold a plebiscite? Why not a sign saying 'Welcome to Rattlesnake Country'? What happened to the old 'Garden of Eatin?'"

Jay is watching for our place across the lake. He turns towards me. "That sign's been here for years. This is wine country! Grapes have been grown commercially here for almost a century. It's not just a name game. Places change. Who knows? The next crop could be solar arrays."

"Maybe you're right, " I lament. "But it's happening so fast! Who will remember the original landscape?"

Jay laughs. "What's your problem? You sound like a Whinery!"

"The price of land has skyrocketed." I'm on a rant. "'Wine country' is just another way to market this place.".

"But that's happening everywhere. Besides, what's wrong with that?", he quips. He tilts his head towards me and raises his eyebrows, " Maybe you just don't like the look of vineyards, the crucified vines with the espaliered branches." He pauses, "Although, come to think, they've been doing that with dwarf fruit trees for a while."

Then he winks, "Could it be the bondage thing?"

I don't respond.

Jay raises his shoulders and his voice, "Look! Wine country is an idea whose time has come. People have been growing grapes here since the 1920's! People make a living at this. Wine is a product we consume. And it's local!"

He pauses, then grins, "You know, I bet we could do this! I can see it now:

BLACK BADGER WINERY

is one of the undiscovered gems of the South Okanagan valley.
Nestled on the eastern side of Okanagan Lake under the cliffs and canyons of Okanagan Mountain Park, our grapes are surrounded by neighbouring vineyards and orchards that have been nurtured under family stewardship for generations.

Black Badger is a natural winemaking niche!

In this locale, long hours of direct sunlight and the moderating influence of the lake combine with the rich glacial soil of the North Naramata Bench to produce wines rich in flavour and aroma.

Wikipedia: 'A pied a terre is a small second home in the city (typically an apartment or a condominium). It has connotations of a jet set life-style ...The phrase literally translates to "foot on the ground." This is said to be because pied a terres were traditionally ground-floor apartments.

However, more likely, the meaning of the phrase is "to have a foothold," cf. "one foot in the grave"; "terre" (ground) referring to (a different) territory, rather than elevation.'

Hmmm. Maybe this place is my pied-a-terre. But is it my main squeeze? Is it the locus of my longing? All homes on this planet used to be pieds-a-terre, grounded in the land. Maybe this is my "coeur-a-terre," because it's saturated in sentiment? Or a "terre-a-pied" because you have to hoof it by foot?

❧

In the language of viniculture, this valley is "terroir," the sum of the grape's environment, its soil and temperature and shade or sun exposure, its elevation, rainfall. Its home.

At this very moment all over the earth, vines curl and grasp their way into fruit. They drill into the soil and corkscrew into branches, tendrils of fruit-bearing stock waiting to be pruned and trained, hardwired to planet earth.

In Napa North, we're up to over 130 wineries.

~~EUROPEAN~~ OKANAGAN ~~WEIN VIN~~ WINE

Pinot Gris	Pinot Blanc
Chardonnay	Cabernet Blanc
Sauvignon Blanc	Syrah
Ehrenfelser	Rose
Meritage	Merlot
Gewurztraminer	Cabernet Sauvignon
Pinot Noir	Petite Verdot
Chenin Blanc	Malbec
Riesling	Ice Wine
Vidal	Auxerrois

Viognier	Pinot Noir
Cabernet Franc	Gamay Noir
Marechal Foch	Zeigelt
Pinot Grigio	

The new fence at Paradise Ranch is a high-wire act, 12' high, posted, and electrified. The sign on the gate reads: "Private. No Visitors. No Public Access. Okanagan Vineyards Family Estate #31." The fence restricts the flow of wildlife to the ranch, especially from Okanagan Mountain Park. It is intended to protect the grapes, by restricting access to bears and other animals. This keeps the staff from "having to shoot them." Now we're officially a Gated Community

The Ranch has been bought and sold several times in the past half century, shifting from Wilsons' family ranch to large scale agribusiness in decades. More than one hundred acres are cultivated in grapes. The lower fields, winter groomed in alfalfa when we arrived, are now greened with grapes. At the end of the summer when the harvest is ripe, propane-charged "bear bangers" cannon the autumn air at dawn to scare away birds, bears and other critters. By October it sounds like a war zone.

❧

When we moved here, the Okanagan Valley was a mirage, an illusion, a hothouse Brigadoon of liquid open lake and threadbare, dry hills. Living at the end of the road in a cul-de-sac meant that we wouldn't be a drive-by to somewhere else. People wouldn't live here if it meant half an hour's drive just to buy a litre of milk.

Nowadays they'd run!

I'm not kidding. The Penticton Ironman triathlon attracts contestants from all over the world, but now even locals bike and run along the

Naramata Road. Extreme sport athletes – climbers and skiers and cyclists somersaulting rock cliffs – have replaced orchardists and 120-hour harvest marathons.

Our friend James is back for a visit. He's looking through a Western Living magazine with photos of minimalist architect-designed Naramata homes with one pine tree, a rock, tile floors, and stark furnishings. There are no people in the pictures. No marmots either.

"Well, the valley is starting to look different. They've shut down the Naramata packinghouse. Not enough fruit crop," he says. James lives in Saskatchewan. "I went to look at our old orchard. All the trees are gone. Now it's all grapes. You know, it costs over $10,000 an acre to do that!"

"Did you check their website?" I ask.

"Yup! Their chardonnay sells for $65 a bottle." James shakes his head and grins. "Guess we were in the wrong business."

I pull up the Regional District of the Okanagan Similkameen (RDOS) website.

POPULATION GROWTH OF OKANAGAN & SIMILKAMEEN VALLEYS 1976-2026

Year	RDOS	Okanagan & Similkameen Valleys
1976	52,674	173,592
2006	86,932	352,225
2026	109,066	485,021

ADAPTED FROM: STRATEGY TO ACHIEVE GREEN SUSTAINABLE ECONOMIC DEVELOPMENT IN THE OKANAGAN-SIMILKAMEEN VALLEYS, WESTLAND RESOURCE GROUP, FOR THE RDOS.

"So," James flips down the screen. "by 2026, there will be twice as many people in the South Okanagan as in 1976, when I lived here."

"And if you include the entire Okanagan," I reply, "population will have just about tripled. In fifty years!" I sigh. "Most people would see growth as the driver of economic prosperity..."

James interrupts, "Yeah, they call environmentalists 'Prophets of Doom!' But people just don't want to face the long-term consequences of growth. Has there been an increase in natural resources? What about water supply?"

I chuckle: "People are too busy with the profits of doom!"

❦

The bonsai pine tree in front of the house has faded to rusty-red. We've watered it, hoping to fend off the outbreak of pine beetle, but its needles are dropping. Next year, this tree will have been swooped away by wind, shattered. Nobody will remember this view of the lake, fringed with soft-spiked, wispy needles, floating in the almost-breeze. This tree was the hallmark of this place, growing from rock into sky. We thought it would last forever.

❦

British Columbia is currently experiencing the largest recorded mountain pine beetle outbreak in North America. BC has 12 million hectares of lodgepole pine forest primarily in the Interior.... Projections suggest that approximately 80 per cent ... will be killed by 2014.

– LORRAINE MACLAUCHLAN

In April, 2007, in the Penticton auditorium of Okanagan College, Lorraine Maclauchlan, entomologist for the Southern Interior region for the Ministry of Forests and Range discusses the impending beetle invasion. Lorraine buzzes with enthusiasm. Bugs! Bugs! More Bugs! Photos of northern B.C. flash on the screen, forests of red and grey, as if we're looking through the wrong film gel. She describes how the combined attack of the western and mountain pine beetles, in conjunction with warmer temperatures, has propelled the beetle invasion south from Kamloops into Kelowna and the South Okanagan. Lorraine admits, "Of course it will be a changed landscape."

There's not a lot you can do about bark beetles. Jay buys verbenone strips at Art Knapp's for the big ponderosa off the front porch. It costs $40 for just one package with two patches of pheremones. The directions say that they are only effective for six weeks!

Grape vines aren't susceptible to bark beetle.

From the front porch, the man and woman look out to benchland peninsulas, orchards stretching like fingers into the lake. Sage and bunchgrass shimmer in the margins, while pillows of green trees are embroidered with fruit, like a sampler from a century before.

The balding guy with the grey beard melts into the plastic chair. "The other day I was over at Dennison's, talking to some of the guys I used to know. Nobody talks apples any more. It's all grapes. If you have grapes, people *cluster* around you."

She doesn't respond.

He strokes his beard. "You're just jealous that we never planted grapes."

Everything in front of them is shrivelled-up: the saskatoon, the mock orange, even the pines twist from the relentless heat. The woman holds her wine glass to the light. She takes a sip, then licks her lips. " No, it's not *sour grapes*. I still think that wine-tasting is pretentious and artificial."

The bald guy sits forward and gestures across the rock outcrop. "Just think! If we had a small vineyard..." He raises his hand in a wine-sipping pose, lightly fingering the glass:

"*This pinot gris brings tears to the eyes. Its unique bouquet blends deer mouse droppings with cistern-raised Kokanee, melded with the aroma of rattler and heightened by a twist of pack rat pee. This eclectic blend goes well with any meal, but especially Okanagan fusions of marmot stew, mule deer sashimi and skink en croute.*"

❦

The woman who went back to the city thirty years ago but could not really leave, looks downhill towards the lake. Twenty years ago, Peters bought a piece of land, flattened it and planted grapes. Now they want to cash out and move to Cherryville, where land's cheaper. Nobody will remember that this piece of land used to rise and fall like a bell curve. Where there was sagebrush, now there's a vineyard.

The woman talks to herself. "How can you just bulldoze the place, plant grapes, and sell to the highest bidder? Will anyone remember hoodoos and cliffs and how the place used to be?"

Sometimes this woman acts pretty citified. She wants it to stay 'the way it was', but then she doesn't live here all the time. She knows how tough it is for people to hang on to this place. She knows it's not cheap to subdivide. Margie, her neighbour, figures it would cost a lot to develop - you have to apply for rezoning, and get it approved, and have it surveyed, and get approval for water and road access and health clearance and jump through all the hoops with the Regional District.

She knows about those hoops.

Last week she applied to have the property rezoned.

Bansai fir.

❦ 19 ❦
Solo Dancing

*"It is a strange thing, but I believe being much alone makes me more courageous.
I have been wondering if it is simply from force of habit - or if the spirit really
grows stronger in solitude.*

**– HOBNOBBING WITH A COUNTESS AND OTHER OKANAGAN ADVENTURES:
THE DIARIES OF ALICE BARRETT PARKE 1891-1900**

My life is a study in dualisms: Vancouver/Naramata; teacher/student;
Power Point/ No Point. Next year's fall schedule has been finalized:
Monday mornings my body will spring from bed, catapult into the car,
grind across town, tramp up the industrial stairwell of the College, mosey
down factory-beige hallways, and crimp into an office the size of a walk-
in-closet. Five minutes later, briefcase swinging, papers in hand, I will
pad back down the hallway and into a vinyl-clad classroom, #2400, or
#3680, or #1560, with six tracks of fluorescent lights and five rows of
desks. Concrete walls. Sometimes no windows.

Let's see, Monday night I won't get home until almost midnight.
That means I won't get to sleep until 3. Wednesday, I should take the bus
and Skytrain – that means leaving home early. Thursday, I have another
night class, which means 5 hours between classes. I can get some preparation and marking done then. And go for a walk. I haven't taught two

night classes for a couple of years. Maybe I need to change my schedule.

Can I really do this? What about that erratic heartbeat in the morning? And the headaches after class?

Maybe I can't do this anymore.

I've been thinking about retirement for years. "Re-tirement" sounds like retreads; as if it's a repeat of something you've already done. I understand the tired part – the worn-down, worn-out sense of work. My colleagues would call this 'burn-out', but I've felt this way for a long time. I'm losing my spark! The evangelical part of teaching - the stand-up improvisation, the messianic mix of newscasts and podcasts and text-book material, the forging of current events and daily life into "teach-able moments" – is harder to perform. And at the end of class, when the audience fades away, there's nobody left in the theatre. Just the magician, with nothing in the hat.

Maybe it's always been this way. What's new is my declining health - the rising blood pressure and the headaches. But I can't afford to quit. It's my job! I've only been at The College for 15 years. My pension will suck, and I'll revert to being a housewife.

I send my notice of retirement to Human Resources on May 28.

Mid-November, 2006, I am in 'transition' at the Granite Farm, trying to figure out how and what to do next. My first two pension cheques make it clear that I need to find work, but this is probably not the best place to do that. It's hard just to be here, tromping up and down the hill, hauling wood, and working on the path. I'm not really sure why I've come. Maybe I'm searching for a new perspective. Or even an old one, trying to rekindle the enthusiasm of 30 years ago. I'm still not looking for redemption.

Outside, the bunchgrass clusters against a grey sky. With my arthritis, I can't carry firewood or dig on the road; it's harder to just get up and down the path to the car. I inhabit a landscape of obdurate, scaly rock and a body of blue-veined, brittle-boned parts. The waterfall trickles down the canyon face like a Rorshach test.

Jay phones me every day. The kids call to make sure I'm not 'bushed.' I've put up birdseed: black sunflower seeds; finch food suspended from the pine tree in front; mixed seed in the old feeder to the left of the front porch; a small dangling chickadee feeder by the path. A block of suet hangs from an aspen branch, next to an enormous sunflower head and a birdfeeder.

But nobody comes to visit.

I'm out for a walk with the Naramata hiking group, composed mostly of newcomers and retired people. We head up Gulch Road as a covey of quail scatter from the Oregon grape into the rabbitbrush. Kirsten turns towards Bella, introducing me: "Melody is an old-timer," she says.

Carol has agreed to let me come to choir practice. It's 9:30 on a Tuesday night, mid-November. We sway back and forth with the three-quarter beat of the Christmas waltz.

"... and we wish you-oo-oo-ooooh a goo-ooood year toooooooo."

Carol wraps it for the night, her arms rounding to a full stop. "All right, that's it. Now, we've gone over the schedule..." Big square glasses frame her eyes as she scans the room. "I'll see you next week at the

United Church in town for practice. 7:00! Early! Now, be quick. We need to do an audition, and I need to go over some of the pieces with Sandy ..."

An audition. Could that be me? People scatter out of the room, as if the plague were coming. I haven't had to audition since I joined the university band in first year.

Carol sits at the piano and motions me over. "Nowadays, everyone has to audition." Sandy, the pianist, is at the back of the room, next to Bertie and Jack and Diane. I'm not sure what they're doing here. Holy guacamole! No script, no preparation, no post-structural analysis. Carol's hands dance up the keys.

"Let's try scales. La la la la la la la la."

I sing along, up and up, octaves higher and higher, stretching ... "La la la la la la la la."

"Your range is quite high," she notes. "Now let's have a go at Oh Canada."

Oh No! I don't remember the words! And nowadays it's bilingual. Carol sings along with me, "Oh KaaaNaDaaaah. Our home and nay-tive land."

Just whose home and native land? Not everyone would agree about this....

"True patriot love ..."

How do we love this land? Let us count the ways...The words come from nowhere, pour out, as I fling my arms wide before my audience, "with glowing hearts, we see thee rise, the true north strong and free ..."

This is the Sound of Music!

❦

Carol gets up from the piano bench and stands next to me, facing the jury. "I think the main issue is commitment. How long will you be here? Can you be here for all the concerts? For the practices?"

I'm waffling. How much is enough? How long can I tough it out? Where can I get a job? Where do I belong?

"I was planning to come back up in March," I say.

Diane, at the back of the room, says, "How long will you be here? Can you get the new music before you leave, so you can practice?"

"I'll be here until New Year's and come back in March, once the snow's gone. I'll practice! I'll be ready for the spring concert."

I sense a reluctance in the room. If you can't commit to us, we can't commit to you. You'll have to take a stand. Are you here?

"I really want to be in this choir," I add. "It sounds great, after all these years."

After a pause, Carol turns to me and smiles, "We'll try to make this work."

On my way out the door, Bertie calls out, "You're such a ham."

Climbing up the hill, the flashlight cuts a tiny tunnel of light through the darkness. I left the outdoor lights and Christmas lights on at the house. Their tiny aura of light hangs overhead like a fog, barely visible as I huff up the hill. At least the bears should be hibernating by now. And I don't have to worry about snakes. I try to slow down, to look at the stars. That's Orion's belt, south of Penticton. I breathe deeply, but I'm too scared to slow down enough to really look.

I phone Jay in Vancouver. "I'm sorry to break this to you, honey..."

"What? What's happened?"

"I've made a commitment to the choir. I can't come back to Vancouver. You can come with me to Yakima for the spring concert. And I promised I'd be here for the Centennial Concert next November."

He laughs. "Next November? People will ask where you've gone, and I'll have to say that you've joined the Naramata Choir. You've taken up with a cult. I'll need to deprogram you."

After a morning hunkered over the computer, I go for an afternoon walk, climbing the rocky bluff overlooking the lake; I return from the other direction, picking my way downhill and back toward the house.

This place is a study in contrast. One moment the universe is golden, the next, the sun has dropped behind a shroud of clouds, and the warmth drains from the hillside. Back in the living room, I feel as if I am still outside, connected to the free-form furniture of juniper, currant and pines. The walls have melted away and the place is wild again.

But in the next moment, the house draws itself into being and frames views of the lake, antelope brush and the ponderosa out front. I am inside. The land is outside.

How does this happen?

By the fall of 2008, the scar from my hip replacement reminds me of Chute Creek - it burrows into my flesh, then bulges out below in a darker deep pink ribbon. Standing before the mirror a year after the surgery, it forms a question mark. As the nights grow longer and crisper, I worry about slipping on the frozen path. I'm beginning to wonder how long I can stay up at the Granite Farm by myself.

By the fall of 2008, the scar from my hip replacement reminds me of

But at Art Knapp's end-of-season sale I purchase two cherry trees, a sour cherry and a bing, for seventy percent of their original price. "It's time to resurrect the garden," I tell Jay on the phone.

"The garden" is a 1200' square of land that looks like a dilapidated prison yard. Its border patrol of upright 20-foot poles tilts into the soil at odd angles. We dug and planted this garden thirty years agao before

Phoebe was born. The garden is located 200 feet downhill from the house – out of sight, over the cliff, down the path, and down the road, a 20-minute steep walk from the house in a pocket of knee-deep soil. We abandoned it when we moved to Vancouver. All the fruit trees we planted then have long since died, except for one gnarly apricot.

Jay is silent. He knows that this is a bad move. But he loves cherries. "All right, I'll rig up an irrigation line next time I'm up," he concedes.

The garden fence was designed to keep out 'critters', but the poles are rotten, drooping every which way, and the anchor fence hangs loosely, wavering around the edges. We never did get around to putting in a gate. An elephant could walk through the opening.

We lug the new trees to the old garden site, and Jay drags old pvc pipe up and down the hill. By mid-September, I'm irrigating the new orchard.

"This is crazy!" says Jay, refitting and tightening hose connections, up and down the hill for about the tenth time. "This means we have to be here to water these trees.!

"Yeah, but we'll have organic cherries," I counter.

" How do we get them back up to the house to process?" he asks. "Not to mention what we'll do about bears, and birds. And what about preserving the dryland ecosystem?"

I nod. He's right on every count. And there's more. "I was talking to Dan this morning," he adds. "He said that Bings split. We should have planted Lapins."

I can't figure this out what has come over me. Am I avoiding returning to work? Am I just taking the financial crash and energy crisis seriously?

This garden is rugged and improbable, I don't even have the energy to walk up and downhill to water the trees, let alone do any gardening! When Jay comes up for Thanksgiving, a new sign hangs on the fence.

NORTH NARAMATA RESEARCH INSTITUTE
GRANITE FARM DIVISION
CERTIFIED OENOLOGICAL NICHE
FUTURE SITE OF BLACK BADGER WINERY

❧

The liquid song of a canyon wren, *Catherpes mexicanus*, burbles down the mossy rock cliffs in back of the house. The bird darts around to the front porch, and warbles from the railing. I dash outside, and begin psshhing to draw it near. Suddenly a deep throat of sound pours from its tiny white breast, a song that trickles down like a waterfall. Sibley notes that wrens seem to prefer low, shrubby habitat, often in ecotones, the transition zones between ecosystems. Me too, little wren.

It's mid-September, and our daughter Phoebe comes up for the weekend. She's in the house studying, while I play outside with my new recirculating pond. A familiar sound filters through the air, indistinct at first, then louder and louder. Gurgle, gurble, glurk, gllucck, glaaakkk, ggllurk, glurk.

"Phoebe! Come quick! It's sandhill cranes!" I run towards the lake, scanning overhead.

Crack! The screen door slams shut. Phoebe adjusts the old cloudy binoculars, the ones that went through the wash twenty years ago. Way, way up, is a wavery line of cranes that positions itself into a V-shape, a distinct chevron, and flutters off in several strands. Heading south.

Migration. For sandhill cranes, home is not a destination resort. Home includes the coming and going. It is the hug of the earth to sky through a topography of mountains and rivers, deserts and open space; home is the journey.

And then they're gone.

Sic transit gloria mundi.

So passes the beauty of the world.

♥ 20 ♥
Bedrock

As Thoreau said...what we need now is a culture that deeply loves the wild earth.

– JACK TURNER, THE ABSTRACT WILD

My homing 'instinct' heats up like a Geiger counter as I skirt the Naramata turn-off, drifting down and around that unbanked corner, past fewer houses, more sagebrush, and into open countryside. The road swoops down over the lake on a long straight of way, past the burnt umber pictograph of the Indian Rock, around Rayner's corner past the freshly painted sun/flower boulder, then Hart's Pond. I'm past the cattle guard and over the creek, thicketed in vine maple, drawn down to a whisper of moisture.

Once through the gate, the car flounders up the silty road. At the falls, I drag out my bags – the food that has to go in the fridge, and the computer – and tread up the path. After the first switchback, I'm already out of breath. My heart thunders.

"Pahhnk!" The chevroned shoulders of a nighthawk oar the skyline. The bird plummets to earth with an end-of-the-world freefall groan, to start all over again.

Just south across the jagged cleft of creek, past the big bunion of rock bluff, Harris grandchildren bounce like astronauts on their trampoline in the no-gravity zone of childhood. Where will their lives take them? How will this place stay with them?

❦

"STOP!" Jay yells. "WATCH OUT! A RATTLER!"

A rattlesnake whiplashes downhill just ahead of me on the curve of the path, in the beacon of my headlamp. It sidewinds the fall-line, slipping downhill and off the path in front of me

"I almost stepped on it!" shouts Jay, headlamp scanning the trail above with his headlamp, like a Cyclops. "I turned around to check on you, and I didn't even see it!"

It's late September, and Jay has picked me up from choir practice. In the black-out of night, I scan the dried-out antelope brush and withered saskatoon along the path, but the snake has disappeared. We haven't seen one all summer.

"I guess they're not hibernating yet," Jay adds. The waterfall sputters in the background. He turns and continues more slowly uphill. We're almost in sight of the house. The porch light beacons.

"OH NO!" he yells. "STOP! Here's another one!"

Uphill and between us, another big rattler coils under the rock face. Jay slipped past it before it could coil into an alert, but I'm stuck. It's too close for me to walk past. I can't go beneath the path, because the hillside drops off steeply.

In the spotlight of our headlamps, the rattler looks like a cobra. Coiled, its rattle buzzes. We are mesmerized.

"They must be out hunting. You should be all right, if you continue slowly," Jay suggests. "Just stay to the edge of the path."

Should be isn't good enough. The path is only a foot wide. I am grounded by fear.

TRRRRRRRR, BZZZZZZZZZZZ, RRRRRRRRRRRRRRR.

After about 5 minutes, I slowly, steadily slink past the snake.

❦

Since we moved to the Okanagan Valley thirty-five years ago, this place has been "home," even in my absence. Children would grow up and leave, jobs could end, friends would come and go, but the land wasn't going anywhere. To sell this property would be a renunciation of faith, like giving up a sacred trust. I inhabit, with my neighbours, a unique and vulnerable geography. The tragedy of this commons, is not that we do not get along with one another, but that we are flourishing like weeds, the ultimate invasive species.

Because how uncommon: the wavering thread of sandhill cranes above the lake; angel hair nests of black widow spiders in the basement; the headbobbing clucks of ruffed grouse, chicks bolting like gunshot; the springtime curl of buttercups; the ziggurat of elk silhouetted atop the bluff, the white-throated burbling of a canyon wren.

❦

I have lots of questions. Can anyone speak for a place? How long do you have to live there? A year? Twenty years? Do you need a family pedigree that goes back generations? What counts most towards authority of place – ancestry, crops, hard work or bird lists? Whose version is most authentic?

I didn't live here when the lake used to freeze over and you could drive across it. Nor when the benchlands were dry, before orchards and irrigation, like the old Stocks photographs hanging in the bank. I don't remember trains on the Kettle Valley Railway either. When labourers broke this rock for the railway a century ago, my grandmother had just immigrated to Montreal.

Most of us are more recent settlers. Some only know the place by drive-bys and vacations. Can you know a place if you're only there 'part-time'? Sometimes I'm in Vancouver watching the rain and I imagine clouds floating east and turning to snow, sifting onto the sagebrush in soft wispy silence. And I'm here.

When I first moved to this place, I never felt like I belonged. Now I've been here long enough to convert apples to grapes, reliquish my kids to the city, fight over water with my neighbors, make new friends, and almost lose the land.

Life here is shaped by the elements. Earth. Wind. Water. Fire. This year's brown pine needles, the ones near the end of the branch, blow off on the gusty days when new fronts pass through. Right now, peach-pink Kokanee trout are spawning in Darke Creek, already bleached to grey and white. Ghost trout, they are just able to swim in a holding pattern against the flow of water. How much effort does it take to resist, to stay still against the current?

This is a story about how you move to bedrock and how it does not move to you. You dream about it, plant trees and beaver at it, lug polyethelyne water pipes, looped around your shoulders in lollapalooza rings, up and down creekbeds and across rocky ledges and through the barbwire of knapweed, listening for the chatter of rattlesnakes in the crackle of this year's withered balsamroot. Each time you leave, you close the front door tight – against wind, or packrats or bears – pack out the garbage, lock the gate at the bottom of the hill, and try not to look back. It's the same lonesome, dried out place when you leave as when you came, a little worse for wear, for your having messed with it. The place doesn't even notice your going.

Even while it trickles through your fingers, it grows on you, like the ponderosa out front with the boa constrictor tap root that muscles moisture from rock. Your body roughens and withers, your eyes squint and crease, your creaky hips rock up the path like an old bony horse and you become the place.

When you're away, the out-of-nowhere divebomb earthbound sound of nighthawk swoop makes you home-sick, fed up with traffic and sidewalks, yearning for the smothering heat of summer sun, or even the iced-up-pipes of winter when you have to haul water from the creek. The quiet. The loneliness.

The place doesn't notice when you've come home. But you do.

Granite Farm cabin.

The type used in this book is Joanna, a unique serif typeface designed by the English
author and artist Eric Gill (1882-1940), and named for one of his daughters.
Gill described Joanna as "a book face free from all fancy business," and chose it for setting
An Essay on Typography, his book on type and page design. Supplemental text is set in
Gill Sans, another of his typefaces. The floret ornaments are Celestia Antiqua.

This first issue of Up Chute Creek was printed
in a limited edition of 500 paperback copies
numbered and signed by the author
of which this is copy *271,*

THE OKANAGAN INSTITUTE IS A GROUP OF CREATIVE PROFESSIONALS THAT
HAVE GATHERED AROUND THE GOAL OF PROVIDING EVENTS, PUBLICATIONS
AND SERVICES **OF INTEREST TO ENQUIRING MINDS** IN THE OKANAGAN. WE
PARTNER WITH INDIVIDUALS, ORGANIZATIONS, INSTITUTIONS AND
BUSINESSES TO ACHIEVE OPTIMAL CREATIVE AND SOCIAL IMPACT. OUR
MISSION IS TO IGNITE **CULTURAL TRANSFORMATION,** CATALYZE
COLLABORATIVE ACTION, BUILD NETWORKS AND FOSTER SUSTAINABLE
CREATIVE ENTERPRISES. WE PROVIDE INNOVATIVE CONSULTATION,
FACILITATION, PROFESSIONAL DEVELOPMENT AND **CREATIVE SERVICES.**

WWW.OKANAGANINSTITUTE.COM